Cambridge Handbooks for Teachers

General Editor: J. W. Adamson, B.A.

THE TEACHING
OF
HISTORY

THE TEACHING
OF
HISTORY

BY

EUGENE LEWIS HASLUCK

M.A., F.R.Hist.Soc.

CAMBRIDGE

AT THE UNIVERSITY PRESS

1920

CAMBRIDGE UNIVERSITY PRESS
Cambridge, New York, Melbourne, Madrid, Cape Town,
Singapore, São Paulo, Delhi, Mexico City

Cambridge University Press
The Edinburgh Building, Cambridge CB2 8RU, UK

Published in the United States of America by Cambridge University Press, New York

www.cambridge.org
Information on this title: www.cambridge.org/9781107621893

First published 1920
First paperback edition 2013

A catalogue record for this publication is available from the British Library

ISBN 978-1-107-62189-3 Paperback

GENERAL EDITOR'S PREFACE

THE *Cambridge Handbooks for Teachers* are designed to meet the requirements of "specialist" teachers, more particularly the less experienced, who desire to inform themselves of the recent developments in the modes of teaching their own subjects. They are written by teachers who are conversant with the best thought and practice, and whose chief purpose in writing is to be of assistance in the every-day tasks of the form-room. A school time-table to-day includes many subjects. Keeping that fact in mind, the authors of the various books in the series aim at combining the scholarly with the practicable. While treating their own subjects with the required thoroughness, they will not forget that these are members of a curriculum, that time is also necessary for other studies and that there are associations between the various subjects which constitute any wisely planned course of studies intended to educate.

J. W. A.

February, 1920.

AUTHOR'S PREFACE

SINCE the beginning of the present century a great deal has been written on the subject of the teaching of history in schools. This volume is intended to provide the teacher with some information as to the directions in which improvements in method have been suggested by various authorities, and to indicate the points where recent experiments have accomplished an acknowledged advance on previous practice.

A practical teacher cannot avoid developing a certain bias in favour of some ideas and against others, but it has been attempted in this volume to present the case for each school of method with as much fairness as possible. No attempt has been made to produce a stereotyped syllabus or universal code of rules of method, as it is far too early to decide what will be the ultimate product of the very conspicuous reform movement which is at present in course of development among teachers of history.

E. L. HASLUCK.

HENDON,

February, 1920.

CONTENTS

INTRODUCTION

Why should we teach history in our schools? The question is one which the teacher will surely be called upon to answer at some time or other, very likely as the result of the enquiry of some dissatisfied and unenthusiastic pupil. Many writers have provided answers to the question, and the answers are not by any means similar in all cases. History teaching has been justified on many grounds, some more real and important than others.

The best answer to the question is that a knowledge of history interprets and illumines the whole of human life. We know that the state of affairs which exists in the World at the present day has not always existed; we know that the institutions, the ideas, the States of to-day have not been handed down to us unchanged from time immemorial; and the intelligent mind must from time to time be led to ask how the present state of affairs grew into being and what form the development of human organisation has taken. In a primitive community, such as a tribe of Eskimos or New Guinea savages, there is hardly any need for historical knowledge, for life and manners, institutions and surroundings are much the same now as they were fifty, a hundred, five hundred, a thousand years ago. But in a highly developed State like our own, the need for a knowledge of history is evident, if we are to use our intellectual powers to the utmost. We must know at least how the inhabitants of these islands came to be grouped together as a single organised community, how the present system of common action and mutual protection grew up, how we became possessors of our oversea dominions, why we have been drawn into conflict with other peoples; we shall be led on from this to make similar investigations into the story of the other peoples of that World in which our lot is cast.

This is the main reason why we should teach history in our schools. It adds to our knowledge of the existing state of the World a knowledge of the way in which human society and institutions have grown up, a knowledge without which a modern education can hardly be said to be complete. The same idea lies at the root of two justifications for history teaching with which we often meet. History is said to "broaden the mind" by showing us the conditions, habits and ways of thought of former times, thus not only adding to our store of information but attacking insular prejudices and local conservatism. Again, it is suggested that a knowledge of history explains and illuminates the multitudinous historical allusions that crop up in the newspaper, in literature and elsewhere. It thus opens up a fresh pleasure in literary reading and even in the trivial perusal of the daily news-sheet, not to mention such things as monuments, buildings and street names. The more history a person knows, the greater the results to be looked for in this direction.

Having indicated in general terms what history teaching can claim to effect, we must turn aside for a moment to mention some false and shallow "justifications" of history teaching which, though they are widely asserted, have no sound strength and consequently tend rather to weaken the really unimpeachable claims of history as a cardinal subject of modern Education. A school history-course does *not* provide a training in citizenship; it does *not* constitute a course of training in the study of human nature or applied psychology: and it does *not* make a suitable basis for ethical and moral instruction.

An intelligent voter certainly needs to know something of the past, and a great many psychological phenomena can be studied with more or less profit in the detailed history of certain episodes of the past, but for the political training and psychological exposition derivable from history to have any substance, it is necessary to study the subject in far more minute detail than anyone could possibly find time for in any elementary or secondary school. And from the ethical point of view, there are so many examples of violence, treachery, lying and self-seeking securing temporal gains at the expense of the better moral qualities that to produce a satisfactory effect on the pupil's mind our only course would have to be to adopt the questionable advice by which Plato of old wished to suppress the baser national legends of Hellas and Carlyle in the last century twisted the Machiavellian Frederick the Great into a paladin of Christian virtue. It is not on these grounds that a school study of history is to be based.

The chief complaints that have been raised against the study of history in schools have been provoked by the exceedingly injudicious selection of the matter presented to pupils by the teachers and text-book writers of the past. The pitiable absence of the sense of proportion, the tendency to concentrate on the one hand upon the trivially curious and on the other hand upon the dry summary of names and dates have rendered the old-fashioned history lesson a meet object for ridicule. But present day writers and teachers are gradually being weaned from their affection for the old traditional collection of "facts which mustn't be omitted because they always have appeared in history text-books," and the contents of our modern text-books are beginning to take a form more consistent with a reasonable sense of proportion. The names of Edward II's favourites, the adventures of Richard Cœur-de-Lion in the East, and the domestic chronicle of the palace of Henry VIII are still to be found there, but they appear less on account of their own intrinsic importance than as illustrating the constant struggle between the mediaeval Crown and the Baronage, the great Crusading movement and the great religious struggle between the Protestant Reformers and the old Catholic faith.

Having decided on what grounds, and on what grounds only, history teaching is to be approved, we must next consider the question of what history is to be taught. Now it is impossible to lay down a cast-iron syllabus and declare that it and it alone must be adopted in every British school. Local differences, the time at the disposal of the teacher, the controlling influence of public examinations, the facilities for the study of local history, the opinions of boards of governors and headmasters, the social positions of the pupils, all these things will necessarily modify a school history syllabus. All that can be done is to sketch a general outline and put forward certain principles which may be applied according to local circumstances.

What do we want to teach our pupils? First we must deal with the history of our own country. Then, if the time allows, we can extend the syllabus to include local history and more general history, European or World history. In any case an extension of the syllabus should be made on a logical basis; there is no place for such studies as the history of France, Western Europe, the Severn valley; such divisions represent no definite communities to which we ourselves belong. We are Britons and Europeans, we may be Kentishmen or Cornishmen or Londoners or Liverpudlians, we all share in a common World-History, but we are not Frenchmen or "Western Europeans" or "Severn Valleymen."

Local history, besides often illustrating rather vividly the operations of movements of national importance, is useful for giving local knowledge, and there are not many who seriously oppose its study. European and general history have been more severely attacked, but the school of opinion which declared them to be irrelevant to Englishmen is by now all but extinct, and we need hardly waste time in refuting this obsolete theory.

There are two methods employed in teaching European history as part of a school course. One is to allot special time to it as a separate section; the other is to introduce it casually into the English history course. The latter is objectionable in several ways. It interrupts the course of the English history lessons, it gives only a very spasmodic and distracted account of European development, it leads to a good deal of mental confusion, and it tends to perpetuate the old-fashioned idea of England being the only country whose history has been of real importance in the World. To understand European history it is necessary to trace the development of Europe as a whole, and the scrappy method of dealing with it involved in the latter of these two systems is fatal to an intelligent conception of the elements of the subject. If lessons on European history are intercalated with the general English course, such lessons should be kept separate and should form a continuous series related to one another as well as to the English history lessons.

It is advisable, then, to include if possible a series of European history lessons in our syllabus, and perhaps in addition a series devoted to local history. It is hardly advisable to insert into school courses such sectional studies as constitutional history, military history, or the history of political ideas; we cannot afford time for special treatment of these subjects in an elementary or a secondary school.

The syllabus must be graded according to the capacity of children to grasp the meaning of historical facts. We cannot talk of the State to children who do not appreciate what that institution means. Young children who have not reached their teens rarely have much idea of institutions beyond their immediate personal reach. They know the family, the town, the village, the shop, the tradesman, the post-office, the policeman, the place of worship, the regiment, perhaps also the tax-collector and the election canvass; they know of the existence of important persons like the King, the Queen, the Prince of Wales, the Prime Minister, the leading generals and admirals. But these all seem separate and concrete things in the child's mind; they have little connection with each other, and it is difficult for him to grasp how all these things are bound up together in the organisation of the State.

For the younger pupils, up to the age of eleven or twelve, we can suggest a course more in keeping with the child's knowledge of his environment and his love of the romantic, a course partly social and partly biographical. Some aspects of social history will appeal to the very juvenile mind:—dress, manners, food and drink, sports and pastimes, houses, means of communication, police and the punishment of crime, weapons and military equipment and the development of cannon and ironclads. A great deal of the matter which appears in our social histories is admirably suited for this stage. If a pupil has received a year or two's instruction in this elementary school history before he comes to the age when the more serious history begins, he will be in an immeasurably superior position to the pupil who knows nothing of the social life of the past. Those absurd anachronisms which so frequently make us laugh in reading elementary history "compositions" will thus be reduced to a minimum; we shall no longer hear of Saxon farmers smoking pipes over fires where turnips are boiling, of mediaeval monarchs sending telegrams to Scotland Yard for policemen, or of cavaliers and puritans exterminating each other with lyddite shells and magazine-rifles.

On the biographical side, too, much can be done. All boys and girls love a good story, and if that story centres round a single individual so much the better. Numerous examples could be given of biographies suitable for this stage of instruction:—Julius Caesar, St Augustine, Alfred the Great, Harold son of Godwin, William the Conqueror, Thomas Becket, Richard Cœur-de-Lion, the Black Prince, Richard II, Sir Walter Raleigh, Oliver Cromwell, Bonnie Prince Charlie, Nelson, Wellington, George Stephenson. These are only a few of the more important historical characters whose biographies, simplified and toned down, may well be laid before a class of children of twelve, eleven, ten, nine, or even eight years old. The success or otherwise of these biographies will depend, more than ever, on the faculties of the teacher; it seems hardly necessary to add that such advanced and difficult points as Richard II's Shrewsbury Parliament, Cromwell's "Instrument of Government" or Wellington's strategy in the Peninsular war will be omitted from these simple biographical stories. The examples quoted above are all taken from British history, but there is no reason why other parts of the world should not supply their quota to our collection of romantic celebrities; France can give us Joan of Arc and Napoleon, Germany will provide Charlemagne and Martin Luther, Russia Peter the Great, Sweden Gustavus Vasa and Charles XII, Italy St Francis of Assisi and Garibaldi. Ancient Rome and Greece may furnish us with a score or more of characters, Pizarro and George Washington may be brought from across the Atlantic, while those who happen to be at all conversant with Japanese history may even find a place for Toyotomi Hideyoshi and Saigo Takamori.

The aims and objects of this twofold social and biographical course are, firstly, to raise a preliminary interest in history, and secondly, to provide the pupil with some slight background upon which he can place knowledge acquired later. One point should be most carefully borne in mind; the child should not be taught in a history lesson things that he will have to unlearn at a later stage. Biographies can be simplified without being falsified, and if legendary or doubtful material is introduced, it should be very clearly explained that it is legendary or doubtful. The effect of teaching things that have to be unlearned is particularly harmful, as it encourages the opinion that "History is mainly lies." Though we have the authority of so eminent a man as Mr Charles Kingsley for the truth of this doctrine, we need not pay very much attention to this shallow and rather cheap piece of cynicism. If boys and girls find that what they have learnt as History in the lower forms is largely fictitious, they will naturally be led to wonder whether when they get up to the top of the school they will be told that their lessons in the middle forms were largely composed of imaginative material. Pupils take a keen delight in discovering errors of fact in presumed authorities—they will feel themselves quite superior to Byron and Wolfe when they are told that Napoleon's cannon could not be heard booming through the night before Waterloo and that Sir John Moore was not buried by torchlight—and we do not want to encourage them to shower the same sort of contempt on History as a whole.

We now turn to the work for pupils of somewhat higher age, boys and girls of twelve, thirteen and fourteen, the upper forms in an elementary school and the middle forms in a secondary school. Here we can go a stage further and tackle some more serious history. But we cannot yet set off on a full-blown study of the development of the State. Though our lessons may now take a strictly chronological sequence, we cannot attempt a continuous narrative of the history of the English State. This is undoubtedly a breach with usual practice and tradition. But it may be suggested that many of our difficulties and failures have arisen from an attempt to teach too much in these years. When we ask our pupils of twelve and thirteen to learn the continuous narrative from the days of the Ancient Britons to the reign of George V we are asking too much from them. The idea of History that we should give pupils of these ages is that of a series of interesting episodes and situations, not that of a continuous development, for the juvenile mind has not yet reached the stage at which continuous developments extending over decades and centuries can be properly appreciated. Impersonal things, too, make as yet little impression, and we shall have to confine our outlook to the human element. Thus such things as parliaments, ecclesiastical synods, local government, political ideas, in fact the whole constitutional side of history may be relegated to the future course of study.

To say that we cannot at this stage attempt a continuous

narrative of the history of the English State does not mean that we should either omit to bring out the chronological relationship of the topics selected for lessons or fail to refer back to past lessons for information bearing upon present ones. A rough time-chart ought certainly to be made from time to time to indicate the relative position in time of the events dealt with. And great use can be made of references to things learnt about in previous lessons which help to explain or clarify later events. Thus, in a lesson on Henry VIII and Pope Clement VII which introduces the class to the opening of the Reformation in England occasion may be found for calling to mind things which were discussed in past lessons on the Lollards and on Becket; in a lesson on Joan of Arc we may refer to previous lessons on Agincourt and Crecy; in a lesson on the Indian Mutiny to what we had to say about Clive and Warren Hastings. We must certainly see to it that our pupils do not get the radically false idea that each historical event is something isolated and independent, though it is rather too soon at this stage to attempt to supply that continuous connective tissue which in older forms carries the historical narrative on from point to point as the serial story of one great drama—the development of the nation.

When a one year's or two years' course of this type has been given—two years for preference—the pupil will have a historical background which will lend reality and colour to the more advanced work in higher forms of secondary schools. Should the scope of history be extended before this advanced stage? As regards European history certainly not, except as illustrating and assisting English history; European history is too broad a subject to allow of the minuteness of detail and the wealth of colour here given to English episodes and characters. But there is some scope for local history at this stage, and we may well include, either separately or as illustrations of the lessons on English history, some lessons on the antiquities and the associations of the local town or countryside.

When our pupils have reached the age of fourteen or fifteen, we can commence a third stage of instruction. In this we are able to turn our attention to the more serious study of historical development. Such a study is only suitable for the higher forms of a secondary school, and can hardly be introduced at all into the elementary school. The course here begun may be made to cover two or three or even four years according to the circumstances of each particular school.

Now there are two distinct methods of dealing with the subject in these upper forms. There is the continuous method and there is the concentric method. In the former we start with the earliest times and work steadily forward term after term and year after year until at the top of the school we arrive at the nineteenth and twentieth centuries. In the latter we cover the whole course of English history each year, but in each form we give special attention to some particular aspect of history, political conflicts one year, wars and foreign policy another year, constitutional developments another year. Both these methods have their disadvantages. The chief complaint against the former is that the story of the nation becomes so long and dragged out that pupils on arriving at its conclusion have forgotten the earlier chapters. Again, it is argued that a mixture of all types of history, political and social, foreign and domestic, secular and ecclesiastical, constitutional and military, leads to some confusion of thought and treatment, and that a strict separation of the various sections of history will vastly facilitate learning. Further, it is well known that pupils are impatient to get on to modern times and learn about the history of the generation in which they have been born, and it is said that when contemporary history is relegated to a distant future much of the eagerness of anticipation is removed.

On the other hand there are great flaws in the concentric system. Classes become tired of being kept to one aspect of history for a year, particularly when they come to the more prosaic constitutional section. It is urged that the separation of history into watertight compartments gives the pupil a totally false idea of the subject. The constant covering of the same ground, too, robs the later terms of the course of that air of complete freshness and novelty which are some inducement to interest.

Though there are some ardent supporters of the concentric system, on the whole it must be said that the advantages of the older method are preponderant. The complaint that pupils will forget the early period of the continuous course applies with partial cogency to the early subjects of the concentric course. The impatience of the pupil to reach the contemporary period is a small matter. The confusion and difficulties arising from the mixture of all sorts of historical information is great, no doubt, but there is a way out of this maze which does not follow the line of complete concentricity. This way out may be said to follow a line of partial concentricity, and it is in the details of the course and not in its general outline that the concentric method can be used with the greatest effect. Within the limits of a single term the concentric system is of great value. An example of its application may be given in the history of the period 1603—1689. Now one of the greatest difficulties—if not the greatest difficulty—adherent to the study of this period is the intermixture of two main threads of development, the religious struggle of High Church and

Low Church and the political struggle of Crown and Parliament. Here we have two separate questions being thrashed out for the greater part of a century. Shall the national religion be Puritan, Roman Catholic or Elizabethan Anglican? and Shall the Sovereign or the Houses of Parliament exercise the dominant share of the rule over the country? The questions in themselves are quite distinct and separate, but as they were both being disputed and fought over at the same time and by the same men their history is necessarily very closely intertwined. A very much clearer conception of the permanent results of this important period can be obtained by a separate consideration of the two main channels of religion and the Constitution than by a continuous narrative of the whole contents of the period. But to pursue this method as far as to slice the entire subject of English history down along its whole length into separate strips is both unnecessary and inadvisable. The course pursued must resemble, not so much the rapid ebb and flow of a succession of high tides, as the steady recession and advance of the waves of one strong and slow tide.

The apportionment of the subject to the various terms must of course depend upon the time at the disposal of the individual teacher and the arrangements made for the introduction of other historical material. Where possible, European history should be introduced at this stage, to run concurrently with the contemporary English history. On the other hand, as has already been mentioned, local history finds a rather more appropriate place in the course allotted to the middle forms of secondary schools.

The most satisfactory provision is for a three years' course of English history, for pupils of the approximate ages of fourteen, fifteen and sixteen respectively. The division into three periods must be to a certain extent arbitrary, but there do undoubtedly exist two great dividing-places in our history. The first comes at the great breach with mediaeval tradition at the end of the fifteenth century, corresponding roughly with the reign of Henry VII; the second comes at the great industrial revolution of the end of the eighteenth century and the beginning of the nineteenth. No exact date can, of course, be fixed for the commencement of a great historical era, and we shall find ourselves inclined in some cases to relegate to the earlier period things which did not happen until the more recent period was well advanced. As regards the first dividing-point, the old-fashioned 1485 is hardly satisfactory, as it excludes from the earlier period the Star Chamber and the suppression of the baronial liveries and liberties which make the last chapter of the great mediaeval struggle between the Crown and the Baronage. 1509 or even 1529 are more suitable dates of division; perhaps if we fix the boundary at the close of Henry VII's reign in 1509 we shall have hit the most suitable and convenient place for it.

In the later period the division proves more difficult, for though the forces that were to characterise the new era were already vigorously at work much earlier, the outward forms and policies of the old era were well maintained down to the second and third decades of the nineteenth century. In this case it will probably prove advisable to deal with the old factors mainly in the earlier period and to reserve the new factors almost entirely for consideration in the later period. Thus the political struggles of the first twenty or thirty years of the nineteenth century, down to the sudden bursting in of parliamentary reform to the centre of the political stage in 1830, really belong to the earlier period, and the same can be said for the military and naval events of the Revolutionary and Napoleonic wars. But the development of the new mills, factories and forges, the first great activities of the Industrial Revolution, the building of Telford's roads and Brindley's canals, and the early agitation for Parliamentary Reform really belong to the new period. Perhaps the most convenient dividing-point is the year 1815, for up to that year the national interest was concentrated on old-fashioned politics and Continental wars similar in character to those of the past century, while it was on the termination of the great struggle with Napoleon that the new political influences engendered by the Industrial Revolution first began to make themselves really felt. While fixing our boundary, then, at the year 1815, we can include in the earlier period some events which fell after that date, whilst we can postpone some matter usually introduced into the history-books before the Great French Wars for consideration in the succeeding part of our course.

This gives us three periods for a three years' course:—To 1509, 1509 to 1815, and 1815 onwards. For a two years' course perhaps the most convenient division would be 1603, although this leaves rather more to be got through in the second year than in the first. For those who are enabled and inclined to indulge in the luxury of a four years' course perhaps the most harmonious division would be:—To 1509, 1509 to 1689, 1689 to 1832, and 1832 onwards. But a four years' continuous course of English History is not so suitable to school pupils as the shorter and more compact three years' course above outlined.

The apportionment of the details of the history syllabus will be a matter of individual taste. But in its main outlines it ought to follow the general principles here outlined, the division into graded stages, for lower, middle and upper forms, the variation of the type of work done at each stage, and the final attainment of a fair knowledge of the evolution and development of the history of this country. One word as to a complaint often heard among parents and others. It was formerly a reproach to the teaching of History in this country that a schoolboy never learnt about anything more recent than the battle of Waterloo. Of course no teacher would be so foolish nowadays as to adopt a syllabus which would stop at 1815; and if, by leaving school before they reach the top form, boys and girls miss that part of the course of instruction which deals with the most recent period of History, the fault will now lie with the parent who takes them away and not with the schoolmaster.

Let us turn to the consideration of the question of the selection of material for English history lessons. For it is a most important thing that the teacher should be able to discern the proportional importance of the facts and features of the national history. Far too little attention has as yet been devoted to this question, as a rapid perusal of the numerous text-books published during the last fifteen years will show. Historical writers and teachers have for long been content to repeat the system and statements of older writers of text-books, and conservative tradition has held firm sway. There is a great temptation to attach importance to a question or a fact because we ourselves learnt about it in our own young days. To give a few examples:—Ranulf Flambard is not a character of first-rate importance in the national history, but he regularly makes his appearance in the text-book; Raleigh's Guiana voyage and Prince Charles' visit to Madrid were hardly events of lasting importance, but few books omit them; the great fire of London really belongs to local history but no writer likes to omit it from the history of England; the various Wilkes incidents are all rather trivial, but a great deal of space has usually been allotted to them. It is necessary to revise our historical material with a rather strong critical attitude, in order that we may appreciate the essentials of history and eliminate whatever is of trivial importance.

It will be as well here to enter in some detail into the outlines of English history as they present themselves to a broad and general survey. Such a discussion may seem perhaps unnecessary to many teachers, but if we are to judge by the text-books of the present day and by the almost universal practice in the modern schools it can hardly be said that history teachers as a whole have formed any clear conception of the general framework of the subject.

Our history begins with a period of preparation, a period during which forces are operating to bring about the ultimate establishment of a united English State. In one sense the history of England as a State begins with the establishment of the overlordship of Egbert of Wessex in 827, in another sense it begins with the adoption of the title "King of the English" by Edward the Elder in 900. But in neither case do we have the creation of a really centralised State; for all practical purposes England remains a confederation of principalities until 1066. The ease with which the realm was divided between Canute and Edmund Ironside in 1016, and between Harold and Hardicanute in 1036 points to the imperfect realisation of national unity as late as the eleventh century. It is not until the establishment of the strong centralised government of the Norman kings that the country obtains anything really to be described as unity. Even so the organisation of the feudal estates tended to perpetuate local separatism, and under a weak king there is a marked reaction towards the federal idea, but 1066 certainly does mark a very pronounced, if not decisive stage in the unity of the State.

Here then is our first historical channel of events. The main question in this period is How did the English State come to be formed? We take the earliest foundations. A Celtic people, in a low state of civilisation, is brought under the rule and influence of the Roman Empire. This Celtic race, Romanised by three and a half centuries of Imperial rule, is partly driven out and partly conquered by a Teutonic people, the Anglo-Saxons, and Great Britain becomes divided into two parts, a Teutonic eastern part and a Celtic northern and western part, each part being subdivided for political purposes into a number of separate states or principalities which are soon engaged as often in war with their neighbouring kinsmen as with the racial enemy in the other part of the island. The Anglo-Saxons succeed in establishing their rule over the best and most fertile part of the country, and there follows a gradual development of unity and concentration of interests among the various Teutonic states. The chief factors in this process are firstly the influence of the Christian Church of Rome, secondly the pressure of the invasions of the Northmen, and thirdly the common subjection to the Norman conquerors from across the Channel.

The purpose of this brief summary is to indicate how, by following a logical plan instead of a merely casual chronological arrangement, we can base our history lessons on a reasonable system. The usual method of treating this period is entirely chronological. To take an example from the latter part of it, we usually find the following method of presentment:—St Augustine's Mission, Edwin and Paulinus, wars of Mercia and Northumbria, St Aidan and the synod of Whitby, Northumbrian culture, Mercia under

Offa, Egbert's supremacy, raids of the Northmen, reigns of Ethelwulf and his sons, Alfred the Great, Edward the Elder, the Danelaw, Athelstan, the battle of Brunanburgh, Edmund, Strathclyde and the King of Scots, Edred and Edwy, Dunstan, Edgar the Peaceable, Edward the Martyr, Ethelred the Unready, Danish raids, Edmund Ironside and Canute, Canute's pilgrimage to Rome, Godwin, Harold and Hardicanute, Edward the Confessor, Godwin's expulsion and return, Harold's usurpation, Stamford Bridge, Hastings, William the Conqueror. Now this arrangement of leading topics has one advantage, that of chronological simplicity; we can jog along through the centuries without having to look before and after. But unless the facts herein presented are organised, the real meaning of the history of this period is lost. The true presentment of the history of these centuries will unfold itself more or less on the following lines:—Forces tending to national unity (the Church, the Danish raids, the Norman Conquest); how the Church established itself in England, conflict of two rival Churches, Synod of Whitby, organisation of the English Church, unifying effects of a single Church; how the Northmen came to England, the raids develop into conquests, the climax of the struggle under Alfred, establishment of the Danelaw, its reconquest by Edward the Elder, a period of peace, renewal of the invasions under national direction, the conquest of England by Canute, the collapse of Danish rule, general effects of the period of Danish invasion; the development of the idea of a Norman invasion, Harold's accession provides the excuse, the invasion, diversion at Stamford Bridge, Hastings, submission of the country, suppression of English revolts and completion of the conquest, unifying and other effects of the Norman Conquest. We are here pursuing a definite logical plan; the story is no longer a disjointed series of successive reigns and notable occurrences, it is an organic whole; it is not a string of beads but a solid and connected piece of work; it resembles no longer one of those worms that can be cut up into a series of separate and still living worms, but a vertebrate animal whose backbone cannot be severed without vital injury.

To proceed, we come to the period of the later Middle Ages. Now in this period we have five main channels in which our history flows. First we have the channel of feudalism, which forms the basis of what we generally term mediaeval society; then we have the great contest between centrifugal and centripetal tendencies, the struggle of local separatism against national unity, the conflict between Crown and Baronage—the most important factor in the domestic history of this country and of many other countries during the Middle Ages; thirdly comes the adjustment of the claims of Church and State; fourthly we have the development of the Constitution; and lastly there is the expansion of English power beyond the limits of the Kingdom. We are at the present day removed by so many centuries from the Middle Ages that we can review them as a whole, and when we do so these five main channels of history are discernible. Now there may be some considerable difference of opinion as to whether it were better to take each of these channels or threads separately, and follow them throughout their entire length or to proceed more strictly in chronological order and take, for instance, first the initial stage of the Crown and Baronage contest, then the Anselm phase of the ecclesiastical struggle, and then the Norman structure of the Constitution. Different teachers will doubtless come to different conclusions on this question, but it is hoped that it will not be considered too revolutionary if it is boldly suggested here that in this case the concentric method should be applied to the whole history of the later Middle Ages. That period is so far removed from us that we can safely teach it in this way without seeming to get too far ahead with one aspect of our subject. It would hardly be safe to suggest that the four centuries following the year 1509 could be so intelligibly taught in this manner, but the four centuries or so preceding that date can be more briefly summed up as constituent parts of a more or less distinct and homogeneous age.

If we take the Middle Ages in this manner, we shall then proceed to follow out the course of the five main channels here outlined. The subject of feudalism comes first. Here we must begin by explaining why and how feudalism first sprang up; we must then proceed to an account of its organisation under the Norman Kings, the agricultural and economic system of feudalism, the financial system of feudalism, the judiciary system of feudalism, and the military system of feudalism. The advantage of dealing with these important questions as a whole, as compared with the old method of taking them point bv point as they happen to crop up in the chronological narrative, Domesday Book, Flambard's extortions, Henry I's Charter, scutage, etc., is obvious. We can then go on to discuss the causes which led to the decay of feudalism, the growth of the spirit of nationality, the organisation of the new mercenary army, the centralisation of the courts of justice, the growing centralisation of the Constitution generally, the economic changes produced by the catastrophe of the Black Death, the advent of new ideas in the fifteenth century. The devotion of our first lessons on the Middle Ages to some such survey as this will make the comprehension of the rest of mediaeval history infinitely easier.

The struggle between Crown and Baronage comes next.

It resolves itself into four main stages. First we have the period when the Crown is fighting a defensive battle against the aggressions of the nobility, this stage lasts until the great revolt of the barons in 1173 and 1174. Then comes a long period during which the Crown tends to be in the ascendant and when the Baronage entrenches itself behind the ramparts of precedent and constitutionalism, fighting a defensive battle against the Crown. With the conclusion of the first part of the Hundred Years' War there begins a third stage; the Baronage has got into its hands that powerful instrument of offence, the Livery system, and from 1377 to 1485 the monarchy is a mere creature and plaything of the great nobles. The advent of licence to the feudal aristocracy gives rein to internecine feuds which end only in the Wars of the Roses, and this paves the way for the fourth period when, by the aid of the Star Chamber, the Tudor monarchy finally puts an end to mediaeval baronialism.

The affairs of the Church are more suitably awarded a different method of treatment. The position, aims and claims of the great Catholic Church should first be taught. Then we can summarise the different grounds on which Church and State came into collision, concerning the appointment of ecclesiastics, the trial of clergy, the taxation of the clergy by the State, the taxation of the laity by the Church, and so on. These can be further exemplified in detail.

The Constitution, too, will demand a sectional treatment. We can take the Crown first, and outline its prerogatives. We can investigate the important question of the succession, and trace the conflict of the opposing theories of hereditary descent, baronial election, ecclesiastical sanction and parliamentary disposal. Then there is the Parliament, the original Witan of the Saxon kings becoming the Magnum Concilium of the Normans; we can trace how the membership of this body came to be narrowed down to an oligarchical group of nobles and how its doors were opened again by new creations to the peerage. Again, we have the King's Council as a committee of the Great Council, and the whole organisation of the civil service. The origin and development of the Commons will be next presented, the increase in their nominal prestige under the Lancastrian and Yorkist kings, and their gradual rise to the position of a regular and necessary part of the national Parliament. Some space can here be given to the judicial system and to local government.

Finally we have the foreign policy of the realm, which will be found to resolve itself into four great aggressive movements, aggression in Wales, aggression in Scotland, aggression in Ireland, and aggression in France. In each case a consideration of the general course of our mediaeval foreign policy will be found to impress the pupil far more deeply than the jerky treatment of these matters usually followed. If, for instance, Owen Glendower's rising can be presented in its proper logical place, as a late consequence of Edward I's conquest of Wales a century or more before, and if Edward III's Scottish wars can be connected with the earlier struggle of which they form merely the later part, the old-fashioned aim of storing the memory with a long series of disconnected facts will have been replaced by one based on the real meaning and significance of scientific history.

This brings us to the end of the Middle Ages, and we now embark upon the period from 1509 to 1815. There is some difficulty in finding a suitable appellation for this period, for since the great historians of the eighteenth century devised the names Ancient, Mediaeval and Modern to express the eras which had passed over the human race up to their own time, there has been a revolution in the conditions of life which has brought about a greater change in things than occurred between the Ancient and the Mediaeval eras or between the Mediaeval and the Modern eras. Perhaps, in default of other suggestions we may describe the period we are now entering upon from 1509 to 1815 as the Modern Period, while we refer to the age since the latter date as the Recent Period.

Here we come to an age which cannot quite so easily be divided lengthwise. For whereas the great questions of the Middle Ages, the value of feudalism, the balance of power between Crown and Baronage and between Church and State, the national unity of England, the expansion of English power, remain under discussion during the whole age, the great questions of the Modern Period are often either settled half way through the era or not commenced until half way through. For instance, the religious conflict virtually ends in 1689, for the feeble flickerings of Jacobitism never really imperilled the country. The contest between Crown and Parliament, too, is definitely settled in the same year. The expansion of England across the ocean, on the other hand, does not begin until the end of the sixteenth century and the great series of English interventions in the Continental wars does not begin till the close of the seventeenth.

Broadly speaking, we have the following elementary channels of English history during the Modern Period:— The Reformation and its ultimate religious settlement, the conflict of the Crown with Parliament, and the building up of the Empire. The first of these takes us from the breach with Rome under Henry VIII, through the vicissitudes of Edwardian Protestantism and the Marian Catholicism to the medial settlement of Elizabeth, then on through a long stretch of Catholic and Puritan suppression and intrigue to the outbreak of the great religious war in the seventeenth century; there follow the Puritan triumph, the Anglican reaction, and the Church settlement of the Restoration; the settlement is then threatened once more from the Catholic direction, and this leads up to the upheaval of the Revolution of 1688, after which the Anglican Church emerges as the undisputed ecclesiastical establishment of the nation. There is really no great harm done in teaching the whole of this sequence of religious events before going back to the Tudor monarchy and the struggle between Crown and Parliament, though many teachers will undoubtedly prefer to make a break at the establishment of the Elizabethan Settlement in order to avoid too long a series of lessons on ecclesiastical history; for altogether about a third of the History of England during this "Modern Period" will be found to be connected with ecclesiastical concerns.

Then comes the Constitutional question of the relative powers of Crown and Parliament. By the overthrow of the feudal Baronage and the subjection of the Church to royal control the power of the Crown is elevated to a high pitch. There follows a period of personal despotism unknown at any other period of our history, during which the claims of Parliament begin to be heard. The accession of an alien to the throne in the person of James VI of Scotland puts Parliament on its mettle, and there follows a long period of combat between Crown and Parliament, complicated by the contemporary ecclesiastical disputes. The question does not reach a definite solution until 1689, although the acts of the Long Parliament in 1640 and 1641 mark a definite stage of progress. Again it may be suggested that this subject should be dealt with in an organised form, and that we should take the purely constitutional, the financial, the judicial and the military questions under dispute separately and summarise the results obtained by Parliament in each of these fields of action up to 1689.

With the advent of the eighteenth century the centre of interest shifts to foreign politics. But before we embark on the wars of Imperial expansion it is necessary to outline the system under which the country was governed during the period of Parliamentary aristocratic rule. We have to outline the constitution of the House of Commons, the position of the House of Lords, the attacks upon the Revolution Monarchy by the Jacobites, the rise and progress of the Cabinet system and of political parties.

The wars of Imperial expansion may be prefaced by an account of the early American settlements and the Dutch wars of the seventeenth century; it is far more logical that they should come in here than that they should be dragged in chronologically to disturb the narrative of the constitutional and religious struggles of that time. The Dutch wars can be followed by the change of policy towards the Netherlands owing to the growth of the power of Louis XIV of France. We then proceed to outline the main causes of what Sir John Seeley calls the second Hundred Years' War with France, which we can then follow up in some detail, until we at last reach Waterloo and the termination of the long struggle.

The history of the Recent Era now begins. The starting point for this era must necessarily be at the Industrial Revolution. Before this period can be approached it is necessary to devote some time to the story of the development of the great modern inventions and the consequent effects upon industry and commerce. It will be found that this introduction to the period will take much less time to present than its importance might suggest, for it is a simpler matter to sketch the broad general factors of history than the lesser and more changeable which arise out of national, party and personal politics. When this introductory sketch of the Industrial Revolution and its effects has been given, we may proceed to the two main channels of our history during the Recent Era—the growth of democracy and the building up of the British Empire.

Democracy can be taken first; we outline the causes of the growth of the doctrine, its effects on English political life, and its gradual assertion in the affairs of the country. The three Reform Acts lead up to subsidiary measures, such as the Municipal Reform and County Councils Acts, the abolition of purchase of commissions in the Army, the opening of the civil service to competitive examination. There may perhaps follow a brief account of political parties since the Reform Act of 1832. Then come questions connected with religion and with education, questions of special importance to the working classes, such as the Workers' Compensation Acts and the Insurance Act, and measures of more general utility such as the Penny Post and the Drainage Acts. Irish questions can be dealt with to advantage separately and continuously. Foreign policy since 1815 too, should be kept separate as far as possible from the complication of domestic developments.

Finally we have the growth of the Empire. We can briefly recapitulate the growth of our oversea dominions and the development of the Imperial idea. The loss of the American colonies can be dealt with either here or in connection with the French war of 1778 in an earlier part of the course. The chief colonies and British possessions can then be taken in order, and their recent history briefly outlined: Canada, Australia, New Zealand, South Africa,

India. A sketch of the most recent factors of Imperial consolidation and co-operation may fittingly conclude this outline.

Now the foregoing synopsis of the leading features of our history has no intention of pretending to be infallible or prescriptive. It merely suggests the method by which history may be presented to the pupil as a logical and reasonable subject. It displays history as a study in evolution, and its parts fit as clearly and easily one into the other as the various stages of a course in geography, language or mathematics. If some such plan is followed there will no longer be complaints that history teaching presents no real or serious objective or that the study of history has no value.

The preceding remarks have been relative to English history, but the same idea holds good for European history as well, and with even greater cogency. For if the intermixture of all varieties of historical matter in an English history lesson be confusing, what shall we say of a method by which the domestic and foreign policies, not of one country, but of all the countries of Europe, are thus perplexingly intertwined. If the chronological method has been a failure in English history, still more will it be a failure in European or World history. Perhaps an example of the more logical method as applied to one period of European history will illustrate its use in this field.

The recent period in European history presents great difficulties to the student. But these difficulties can be solved if a reasonable method of dealing with the subject is adopted. Recent history begins with the Industrial Revolution in the economic world and the French Revolution in the political world. Before embarking on the history of the nineteenth century the Industrial Revolution should be studied and its meaning appreciated. After the violent effusion of the French revolution and the turmoil caused by the outburst of military vigour which accompanied it, Europe settled down into apparent tranquillity after the battle of Waterloo and the Congress of Vienna. Thenceforward European history has been directed and controlled by the operation of three great forces, Democracy, Nationalism and International Rivalry. In teaching this period, the three forces should be kept apart as far as possible. The progress of democracy can be sketched first of all generally, and then as it occurred in the greater nations of Europe. Similarly, after outlining the aims and ideals of the Nationalist movement, its progress should be traced in large countries such as Germany, Italy, Austria-Hungary and the Turkish Empire, with perhaps some reference to its effects in Poland, Finland, Norway and Belgium. To study the subject in this way is to understand it far more readily than under the old method. Even with international relations we need not stick to a strictly chronological arrangement. We may deal in turn with the great questions which have distracted the Powers during the last century, the Eastern Question, the French danger, the colonial rivalries, the German danger. However much we may ultimately be able to appreciate a continuous narrative of the story, in learning the elements of the subject this simpler method is virtually essential.

Both in arranging his syllabus and in arranging his lessons the teacher should never lose for an instant the general idea of the plan on which he is working. Prominence will be given to the important main channels of history and everything that is unnecessary and irrevelant will be either cut entirely away or used merely as illustrative material. The teacher and the student alike should be able to appreciate what are the essentials of history.

I. THE PRESENTATION OF HISTORY

HAVING discussed why we are to teach history and what history we are to teach, it is now possible to proceed with the methods of teaching the subject. There has been, perhaps, no subject the methods of teaching which have given rise to more discussion during recent years. All varieties of method are "in the air," and nobody yet has propounded a universally accepted system. While a great deal of this uncertainty has arisen from the inability to appreciate the initial facts of what history is really to be taught, another reason for confusion is that many of our well-known history teachers have devoted their attention, and with it their enthusiasm, to some particular section of history, such as social science, source-work, or European history, and have turned their energies into a partial and sectional channel. The ordinary student and teacher will find that to adopt the attitude and policy of a "trimmer" and give due consideration to the claims of all sorts and conditions of historical methodologists will be, not a source of weakness, but the best possible security for a reasonable outlook on the subject.

In former days there were two main methods of procedure. There was the formal study of the text-book, which usually resolved itself into merely "learning" the names and dates. There was also the historical lecture-lesson. These were the methods of assimilating facts; reproduction took the form of oral question and answer, written answer, and lengthy composition. Now all of these old-fashioned methods had their use, and if uninspiring, in the hands of a good disciplinarian they led to some results. They had a good old English hard-working flavour, and as such they compare favourably with some more modern plans. This is not the place for a general disquisition on educational theory, but it may be noted that history teaching has suffered recently from the excessive wave of reaction against the grinding methods of our fathers. A school of teachers, mostly of the rising generation, has appeared which aims principally at "increasing the interest" of the work. This school of opinion has in many cases devised some excellent aids to effective history-teaching, but in its practice of teaching it has led to some lamentable failures. The excursion to the abbey or the picture gallery, the cinematograph film, and the reading from the historical novel will no doubt be vastly appreciated by the pupils, but when the end of the term comes, unless stringent steps have been taken to consolidate and preserve the knowledge thus acquired, the class may be found pitiably ignorant of the period it has been "studying." It might be casually observed that the thick sugaring of subjects like history and geography is a little unfair to the teachers of the more prosaic but equally necessary subjects like mathematics, as it gives the pupil a "spoilt" desire for amusement which will detract from his attention to these other subjects.

The aim of school teaching is not to amuse, nor is it to interest, if that interest is going to be merely ephemeral; in our subject interest must always be a means to an end—the end of gaining a good and lasting knowledge of the outlines of history. Seeing that this must be our obvious aim, our method of teaching must be designed to effect this in the most secure and satisfactory manner. Now it is apparent that the more the brain is exercised over a subject the more lasting will be the impression produced by that subject; hence we must make our pupils use their brains as much as possible in their work. These last remarks are of course platitudes, but it is just as well for some history teachers to be reminded of them.

The main object of the study of history being the acquisition of the knowledge of certain important facts relative to the development of the human race, and of our own nation in particular, we must first enquire what are the most efficient means by which this knowledge can be acquired. The main facts of history can be obtained by reading or by hearing; the text-book and the word of the teacher are the two main factors of instruction in these elementary particulars. Of these two factors the most efficient will be the text-book. An oral lesson may make a considerable impression at the time it is delivered, but the human memory is erratic, and a week or month afterwards the remembrance of the facts learnt will become hazy and blurred. But though facts learnt from a text-book are liable to the same process of distortion and disappearance, the text-book remains as the lasting and visible witness and a source of reference after the teacher's words have become mingled with the air. During an oral lesson, too, individual pupils, through distraction, laziness or absence, may miss some or all of the matter, but with a text-book the same work can be made up after the original lesson is over. The text-book, as containing the essence of the matter under consideration, should be continually kept on the desk in front of the pupil, except, of course, during tests of memory and knowledge. It is important, too, that where possible the school text-book should be carried away by the pupil at the end of the school course, to act as a constant source of reference for historical questions that crop up in the future, or to form the first volume of a historical bookshelf of the pupil's own.

It would be invidious to offer any suggestions relative to the merits or demerits of any of the numerous text-books on the market. A few brief remarks on the points that one should look for in a good text-book are all that can be put forward on the subject. It used to be a sort of maxim at one time, "Small boy, small book." But as a matter of fact, in the history class at least, it is not by any means advisable to proportion the size of the volume to the size or age of the pupil. In truth it might almost be said that we must work here on lines of inverse proportion. It is only an older boy or girl that can grasp the more or less dry facts in a historical summary; your young pupil wants a good thick padding of details and explanation to make his history look intelligible. Generally speaking, then, we should avoid placing a bald summary in the hands of our younger pupils. In the youngest forms, if a text-book is used for social and biographical studies, it should be one that is filled with chatty, descriptive and brightly coloured details. The same applies to the text-book for the middle forms of secondary schools, where the history of England is best taken as a series of remarkable incidents and events; there are very few books yet published which provide a satisfactory basis for the work in these forms. In the upper forms of secondary schools the selection of a suitable text-book will be a matter of very great importance. It must contain all the important facts, but it must not be too long and prolix. It must clearly bring out the relative importance of the facts it contains. It must make some attempt to indicate where the main channels of History lie, and therefore it must not too slavishly follow the chronological system. It must be up to date; antiquated views about important historical events or institutions must not be perpetuated in its pages. It must be brightly and intelligently written, and not such as to repel the interest of the reader. When a new text-book has to be selected in any school, it is always advisable for the teacher to make personal enquiries at some large educational bookseller's and examine a good many volumes before making a final decision. Historical exhibitions, such as that held in the summer of 1914 at King's College, London, afford also a good opportunity for teachers to get into touch with the latest productions in the way of text-books.

When a good text-book is in use, the class should be allowed to use it as much as possible, that is to say, where information may be obtained from the book, the teacher will not provide that information out of his own mouth. The book may be read aloud round the class or studied silently; perhaps the first method is the better, as opportunity is given for an explanation of any words that are unfamiliar to the pupil and for an elucidation of any reference that may be difficult to grasp. The less satisfactory the book, the more call will there be for such commentaries and explanations. It is just as well that before proceeding to any further discussion or illustration of the points dealt with, the matter presented in the text should be thoroughly learnt and mastered, test questions, either oral or written, being given to ascertain that the work has really been done. The task of learning may appear somewhat unpleasant and dull to those whose main idea is to turn a school into a paradise of pleasure, but if anything approaching good results are to be obtained, a good solid grind at the elements is essential.

It may be observed here that it is advisable to give the

pupil a far more thorough acquaintance with his book than is usually done. Boys and girls seldom know the title, author, arrangement, or even the index of their history books. In this last particular it is important that the pupil should receive some instruction. Where it is possible to find out where a thing is by simply referring to the index, the teacher should never tell the pupil on what page it is to be found. It may even prove useful sometimes to set an exercise which will involve an intelligent use of the index; the class may be told to collect all the references to London in the history-book, or to find out on what occasions an English army has invaded Scotland or Ireland, exercises which will accustom the pupil to the use of the index. Of course every pupil should know the difference between an index and a table of contents; a good many do not.

It has been indicated that it is desirable to use a text-book which attempts to organise the facts of history on a more intelligible system than that pursued by the chronological volumes. But in many schools where there is already an established text-book, where books remain school-property, and where there are *no* funds available for renewing the supply of text-books, it will be found necessary to make the best of the old ones, most of which follow the chronological arrangement. Here there is scope for some interesting class-work, for the facts may be selected and sorted from the storehouse of the book, and finally arranged in a systematic order in notes. Thus the class can collect all the material relating to the Church in the Middle Ages. They may summarise each paragraph relating to this subject, and from these notes may be drawn up a compact analysis of the chief causes of dispute between Church and State in the Middle Ages and a statement of the result of those disputes.

There are some who believe that this method is superior to that of studying the organised facts ready arranged in a modern text-book. But although this sort of work no doubt exercises the brain very considerably, it consumes a very large amount of time, and if pursued to any extent it will leave the syllabus time-table in the lurch. There is a certain school of educational theory that advocates an excessive devotion to the "find out" method. In history they are represented by the Source-book enthusiasts; in geography by the Mapping specialists, in Science by the Experiment advocates. A little exercise in primitive enquiry and in the methods of the advanced student is useful at some time or other in nearly all school courses, but to make empirical research the main feature of a school training in any subject is, with its unavoidable sacrifice of time, to throw away the birthright of the rising generation as "the heir of all the ages."

When the selected lesson or subject has been thoroughly mastered from the text-book we can go on to further sources of instruction. Some teachers prefer to test the knowledge acquired from the book by setting questions which require longer or shorter written answers; others will prefer the oral method of question and answer. As a matter of fact the former is more thorough as providing the means of testing the knowledge of each individual member of the class in the whole of the matter learnt. Where questions are asked round the class, the fickle goddess Fortune often plays an important part in the allotment of marks for answers.

Now comes the question of how far the teacher may be allowed to provide information out of his own mouth. The solid backbone of the facts should, as we have said, be obtained from the book. But a very great quantity of expansive and illustrative material can now be provided by the teacher. This may take many different shapes. Throughout, however, the teacher must bear in mind that such information as he gives must be mainly illustrative and should continually refer his observations to the points dealt with in the book. Lecture-lessons, as such, should only be given occasionally; they cannot but be a relaxation of effort for the pupil, and hence they ought to be the exception and not the rule. It has been somewhat cynically remarked that whereas in the old-fashioned school the pupil learnt the lesson and the teacher heard it, in the modern school the teacher learns the lesson and the pupil hears it. This was never so true as in the case of many modern history-teachers. Oral information should be given in small doses; and where a lengthy lecture-lesson is necessary, it should be broken at intervals for the taking of dictated or other notes on the subject under discussion, preferably by way of recapitulation of what has been said.

A good deal of interesting information which combines enlightenment on the subjects under discussion with an addition to the interest of the lessons, can be given by reading quotations and extracts from books. There are many forms of literature which can be pressed into service for this sort of thing. First there are the large historical volume, the historical monograph, and the biography; guide-books, magazines and newspapers occasionally furnish their quota of information; and then there is the historical novel, old or new. A good history-teacher should keep in touch with all forms of literature likely to be of service to him in the teaching of his subject.

An example or two may be given of the effective use of literary sources. A lesson on the Black Death can be added to by a discussion of the subject conducted by the teacher, the reading of Thorold Rogers' account of the plague in his "Six Centuries of Work and Wages," the reading of the introduction to Sir Arthur Conan Doyle's "Sir Nigel," which gives a somewhat impressive sketch of the calamity, the "Statute of Labourers" of 1351, and extracts from the article on Bubonic Plague in the Encyclopaedia Britannica. A lesson on the battle of Waterloo may be discussed with the additional information provided by the personal reminiscences to be found in Sir Edward Creasy's "Decisive Battles," by the well-constructed letters of the Tubney contingent in C. R. L. Fletcher's "Introductory History of England," of the extracts relative to the conduct of Napoleon in Dr Rose's "Life of Napoleon," and the vivid narrative of Erckmann and Chatrian in "Waterloo."

The teacher who makes a point of frequent historical reading will be able to produce extracts and quotations and to provide information from his memory on almost every important event of English history. It is in this respect that the advantage of the history specialist becomes apparent. Given a really good text-book, any intelligent teacher may be able to "keep a page or two ahead" of the class; but when it comes to those discussions and illustrations and exercises upon which the attractiveness and the success of the subject so much depend, the need of a specialist is at once felt. Though some unpractical and "faddist" specialists have failed to produce as good results as a prosaic instructor of all subjects, every secondary school that wishes to produce satisfactory results in this subject will find it essential to employ the services of a specialist teacher in history.

APPENDICES

A. HISTORICAL EXERCISES

WE must now consider what forms of historical exercise can be given to pupils who have had the main outlines of the subject laid before them. These exercises can be of many kinds, and each particular historical subject will probably suggest some particular form of exercise suited to it. A wide-awake teacher will always be on the lookout for fit subjects for exercises, though he must always keep such exercises well within the bounds of his general scheme.

First we have the old-fashioned composition. This is by no means to be rejected on account of its antiquity. In some schools lengthy compositions have been very considerably reduced in late years, with the effect that the arts of writing, spelling, punctuation and the construction of sentences have fallen off very considerably. It is very important, for the general purposes of education, that the art of composition should not be allowed to fall back. In higher forms, where one or more of the public examinations are the goal of the school year, frequent practice in composition is essential. In this case, the teacher will do well to obtain beforehand copies of the recent history papers set in the examinations in question. The past papers of most of our public examinations can be purchased, and a study of a few consecutive years' questions will give a very good idea of the sort of answers that will be required. In the modern public examination in history the questions almost always demand an answer of the composition type, and if pupils are previously trained in the way of readily putting their knowledge on to paper in the form of intelligible sentences, their chances of success in these examinations will be considerably increased.

The composition, then, both for its own sake and with a view to public examinations, will form an important element in historical work for schools. The composition may take several different forms. The higher classes may devote their attention to the straightforward essay type of exercise. In the junior forms it is often an advantage to give the work a rather more romantic and personal interest by turning it into an exercise in which the imagination may have fuller play. A few examples of this type can be given. There is the description written from the standpoint of an actor in the events described. Pupils can be asked to write an account of the battle of Hastings from the point of view of one of the soldiers engaged in it, to write from the standpoint of a member of Parliament a description of the visit of Charles I to the House of Commons to arrest the Five Members, to write the experiences of an English soldier in the war against the Bengalese in 1757 or against the Zulus in 1879. Sometimes it may be possible to allow the members of a class to decide for themselves on which side they will range their imaginary writer; we can tell them to describe either a Puritan from the Cavalier point of view or a Cavalier from the Puritan point of view, or to write about the battle of Bunker Hill from the standpoint either of a loyalist soldier or of a rebel volunteer. Occasionally it is a good idea to ask for both points of view in succession, one in one composition and one in another. Such exercises, in which the powers of imagination are drawn upon and the pupil to a certain extent gets inside his history and for a moment "lives" in the past, are of enormous value in impressing the subject on his mind and stimulating a further liking for it.

Proceeding further, we can devise compositions which do not merely wear the aspect of accounts written by persons who took part in historical scenes but which are written as though they were actual contemporary documents. The easiest form of transition into this realm is the imaginary letter, where an incident is told or a description given in the form of correspondence. Or a letter, fictitious or real, can be written on the blackboard and the class may be asked to write an answer to it from the person or from one of the persons to whom it is addressed. Some of Cromwell's shorter letters demanding stores and giving instructions, taken from Carlyle's "Letters and Speeches of Oliver Cromwell," may be used in this way. Or one can write up an imaginary letter, say, from Burke to Chatham advocating the cession of independence to the American colonies; or from Disraeli to Peel, accusing him of desertion of principle in adopting Free Trade in corn, while we ask the class to write an answer to it as they would think the characters concerned would have answered.

Further, from imaginary letters we can proceed to imaginary speeches. Many suitable exercises can here be given:—A speech of Simon Langton to the barons at Runnymede, an oration of Pym's on the Star Chamber or Ship Money, Marlborough to his English troops at Blenheim, Pitt on the reasons for the war of 1793, Lowe on the Reform Bill of 1867. Again, we can ask for proclamations, an appeal for Royalist or Puritan recruits at the outbreak of the Civil War, a Jacobite declaration of 1715 or 1745, or a Chartist manifesto of the forties of last century. It has even been found effective in some cases to set as a light optional homework exercise the drawing of a cartoon illustrating some political incident of past centuries.

These and such-like exercises will of course be more frequent in the junior than in the senior forms. All such work must be very carefully corrected, anachronisms pointed out, suggestions for improvement made, falsities and irrelevancies struck through. Pupils must be encouraged to bring into their work of this sort as many references to contemporary events and ideas as possible. It is really surprising how a few exercises of this description will stimulate a class, for, particularly in the case of younger pupils, it will be found that a closer and more "personal" contact with historical events will make its members actually keenly excited in passages of history which have formerly left the pupils undisturbed and uninterested.

The next form of exercise that comes to the mind is the mapping exercise. It has been frequently urged upon historical students that one cannot understand political history without having an atlas at hand for frequent reference. It is the same with school work. Good maps must be at hand to explain the movements of political history. We may ask here if it is necessary to have such books as historical atlases for use in class. Now the answer to this question depends entirely on one thing, whether the text-books in use contain sufficient and satisfactory maps to explain the matter presented in the text. As a matter of fact it ought to be very easy to get all the historical maps that are necessary from a text-book. The names of places mentioned in the course of a year's history lessons are not too manifold to include in a short series of maps in the text-book itself. Where European or general history is taken, the same remark applies. But some text-books do not supply adequate maps, and in that case a historical atlas may be said to become necessary. There are several fairly inexpensive historical atlases on the market; these may no doubt be obtainable for examiation on application at any large bookseller's.

Besides having his attention frequently drawn to the map, the pupil should have constant exercise in the reproduction of historical maps, both as a relief from the more usual work of reading, listening, answering and writing, and as an aid to the retention of historical facts. Large numbers of pupils will soon forget the whereabouts of the Anglo-Saxon kingdoms unless they draw a map of them, and the same applies to many other things in history. One important observation may be made with regard to historical maps. They should not contain anything which is not needed for the appreciation of the facts they are intended to illustrate. As always, we must look for the *essential*. It is a prevalent fault of historical maps that they are overloaded with irrelevant details, while they often at the same time omit really important features. For instance, in an ordinary political map to show the extent of States at different periods, it is not necessary to fill in a network of rivers, roads and hills nor to pack in a crowd of towns. Places that are not mentioned in the text, unless they are so important in themselves that they absolutely command insertion, are not required to encumber a text-book map. It is, in fact, often advisable, in maps which merely indicate boundaries or the positions of places unconnected with military movements, to omit physical features almost altogether. In a geographical exercise this would of course be an unpardonable fault, but for illustrating the history text-book it cannot be called to the same account. On the other hand, maps illustrating military movements do require a considerable insertion of physical features, dependent as all military movements are upon the nature of the ground over which operations are being conducted. History books have hardly yet attempted to make use of the modern system of contour-shading for their military maps, yet it is barely possible to understand most campaigns without a contour-map of some sort. This fault is perhaps a little more excusable for general surveys of history which do not go into details of military campaigns, but it is one which is carried into more detailed historical volumes. In any case the maps drawn by our pupils should fulfil the conditions of omitting irrelevant details and including those features which are necessary to the proper realisation of the facts under consideration.

There is a number of maps which must almost of necessity be drawn by pupils—Anglo-Saxon England, the dominions of Edward III and Henry V in France, Scotland to illustrate the Edwardian wars, England to illustrate the Civil War. But many others will suggest themselves both in English and in general history. For local history, too, maps are important, as they help to make the pupil acquainted with his own town and district. One suggestion may be offered in regard to maps which illustrate a continuous narrative, such as that of a military campaign. Instead of making the entire map at one sitting, the pupil should be allowed to build it up as he goes along. Thus in making a map to illustrate England during the Civil War, the outline alone should first be drawn, and then, when the various campaigns are learnt, the places mentioned in each should be inserted, for it will be quite legitimate to interrupt a lesson for the purpose of putting in the name of a place that has some bearing on the narrative.

Map exercises are very numerous, and can be used at the discretion of the teacher. Besides general maps, we can have special local maps to illustrate certain campaigns, plans of battles, plans of towns and districts for local history, and compound maps to illustrate comparisons. Of the latter type we may suggest such exercises as the following:—Show on one map the different parts of France held by our mediaeval kings, or, from a table of statistics show which counties of England gained members and which lost members under the Reform Act of 1832.

After map exercises we come to other forms of the historical exercise. The question of source-work has become one of great interest at the present time, so much so that it demands a separate chapter to itself. Then there are modified forms of source-work which are useful. A few examples may be quoted. The Anglo-Saxon Chronicle gives in considerable fullness the names of the places raided in various years by the Danes; a list of these may be given to the class, and with the names and dates before him, the pupil may be asked to produce either a composition or a map on the subject of Danish encroachments in England. A study of the genealogical trees of the royal families may be made the basis for a series of questions on the succession—When has the hereditary succession been broken? When has female succession influenced the descent of the crown? Compare the value of the Yorkist and Lancastrian claims. An account of the battle of Waterloo may be written from the point of view of one of the combatants by the aid of a large-scale map of the battlefield.

It is impossible to mention all the varieties of exercise which can be utilised in the history class, but a few suggestions may be made which will no doubt lead to others. A great quantity of work is provided in the study of the feudal village. The land system provides scope for a map of the common fields. A lesson on feudal tenures opens up an opportunity for the construction of a rent-roll of an imaginary manor; the names of imaginary tenants may be put down in a list, their status as socman, tenant by knight service, tenant by petty serjeanty, villein, may be indicated, and their rents or services put down in another column. In connection with the military system of feudalism, we can construct orders for the assembly of the military tenants, and notices of the place of marshalling; the local law-court will allow of more exercises in composition, summaries of plea-rolls, lists of fines, notices of days of meeting, and so forth. The position of the Church may suggest other exercises; minutes of proceedings at an arrest of a local "cleric" by a lay official, notes on a quarrel about the presentation to the living of the parish, instructions for the collection of ecclesiastical levies and taxes. If, in the course of a short series of lessons, junior pupils can be got to appreciate in this manner the characteristic incidents in the life of a feudal manor, much will have been done towards the acquisition of the spirit of history.

Let us take another subject—the Revolution of 1689. We may devise all sorts of letters, from King James to Tyrconnel, from Tyrconnel to James, from Sir Edward Hales to his coachman, from Hough to Compton, from Judge Jeffreys to Father Petre. Then we can have a sketch-map showing William of Orange's advance on London, a genealogical table of the royal personages concerned, and a chronological table of the chief events of the Revolution. Proclamations in favour of King James II, William of Orange and Monmouth may be composed, the various suggestions for the settlement of the crown and the distribution of royal power set forth and analysed, and the various reforming changes brought about in the succeeding years by Act of Parliament summarised and tabulated. An analysis and commentary on the Bill of Rights may be made to occupy one or more lessons according to taste.

Another example may be given. The subject under consideration is the Crimean War. First there are the maps, including the Black Sea area, the Crimean peninsula and the environs of Sebastopol. A detailed plan of the Redan can be made, and then may form the basis for a description written by one of the British soldiers who stormed it. A series of bulletins and despatches can be constructed, illustrative of the progress of the winter siege, leading articles may be written condemning or defending the Government at home. A composition may be set asking for a comparison of the Sebastopol siege with the siege of the Dardanelles fortifications in 1915, and an abstract of the Treaty of Paris may be made.

The foregoing examples have been introduced merely to illustrate the various sorts of exercise which can be set in the course of a series of English history lessons. The same sort of thing will be done in European history lessons, where there are similar opportunities for work of varied character. No better idea of the extent of the Roman Empire can be gained than from the following exercise:— An outline map of the Roman Empire is compared with a modern map of Europe and the Mediterranean Basin; the class is then directed to make a list of all the modern countries of Europe which have once formed, either entirely or in part, provinces of the Roman Empire. Again, a few extracts from the historical portion of Machiavelli's "Prince" may form the basis of exercises on the condition of Italy at the end of the Middle Ages. It may also be remarked that short passages from this book form excellent "texts" upon which illustrative history compositions of a general character can be set in senior forms. As an illustration of the variety of exercises to be obtained in this sphere we may quote a few that have been used in connection with the "year of Revolutions," 1848. A series of despatches, sent from each of the capitals of France, Prussia, Austria, Sardinia and Naples, may be constructed to illustrate what was passing in those places, a letter may be written "from Metternich in exile to Prince William of Prussia in exile," and an idealised map of the "free peoples of the Austro-Hungarian confederation" can be drawn.

In fact, the teacher of history will find it advantageous to keep his eyes always open for opportunities for effective exercises of one sort or another. Yet he must never rush at new ideas merely for the sake of novelty; the good old-fashioned composition must still take a prominent place in the work, and care must be exercised that the work done does have some real effect upon the historical knowledge of the pupils. Variation and novelty must, as always, serve as a means to an end, not as an end in themselves.

B. SOURCES

One of the most recent developments in history teaching has been the study of historical sources. In the course of the past fifteen years several books have appeared containing series of extracts from records and documents intended for use in schools. This branch of our subject has been specially promoted in a number of American schools, and there also exists in this country a school of teachers who have been made converts to the method of elementary research. Now although there is much to be said for this method, like everything else it has been overdone in some quarters, and it is necessary to go beneath the surface of the subject and ascertain the basis on which it rests.

First it is urged that the source method gives an insight into the methods by which history has been built up. This is undoubtedly true. Secondly it is argued that the study of sources and the extraction of information therefrom exercises the brain in a very effective manner. This also is true. Thirdly it is said that if we use source-work in languages when we adopt the foreign dictionary, and in geography when we study maps, we should likewise adopt the same system in history.

It will be seen, however, on consideration, that the last argument is somewhat fallacious. What are the methods pursued when we use the dictionary and the atlas? The dictionary is the final product of the labours of a large number of individuals who, delving among the original material of the language in question, eventually bring forth, separated, sorted, classified and polished, a more or less complete list of the words in use in the language under consideration. The atlas, again, is the final product of the labours of another large collection of individuals who, starting with the original soil, rivers, hills, seas and towns, eventually reduce their manifold observations to an orderly and harmonious whole in the shape of a map. When a boy or girl turns to the dictionary to discover the meaning of some Latin or French word, it is not a case of original research but of utilising the research of a considerable number of other people. When the atlas or the large-scale map is set as the basis of a geographical exercise, no research work is being done in the true sense of the term, for the source of the information discovered in this way is the result of the compound efforts and labour of a thousand and one surveyors and cartographers.

Very different is the method pursued by the historical source-worker. He takes as his pabulum a few absolutely original documents, and except for the services of the transcriber and the printer he is indebted to no one for any organisation of the facts. Sometimes spelling is simplified or a foreign tongue translated, but the document remains essentially what it was at first, a bedrock source. From this source the pupil is asked to build up a certain small fragment of history. The work really resembles rather the tackling of a difficult "unseen" than the simple dictionary-method, rather a taste of elementary surveying than of map-reading. The historical document presents only one tiny glimpse into the past, it resembles the photograph of some particular view, and though some documents (such as the Grand Remonstrance of 1641) like views taken from mountain-tops, embrace larger areas of history than others, the majority only illuminate and illustrate certain special incidents and episodes. The true comparison with dictionary and map work would be found when not the source-book but the history text-book forms the subject of research, for here as in the other cases the pupil is using the combined results of the labour of many historical students and writers.

But just as an experience of elementary surveying is good in a geography course, and "unseens" are useful in a Latin course, so may source-work be said to fulfil a useful purpose in a school history course. It is only the extreme claims of the source-book enthusiasts that must be put aside; they would like to make school history teaching mainly a matter of exercises on original authorities, and this is going too far—far too far. An exercise based on a contemporary document may be occasionally useful, the reading of an extract from some contemporary work or document may be often advantageous, but it is not desirable, either from the point of view of time, of the difficulties of archaic and legal language, or of the scrappy and fragmentary nature of such a course, to base our teaching on the system.

A few examples of the good use to which the source-book method may occasionally be put will now be considered. In the "Ancient Laws and Institutes of England," edited by Benjamin Thorpe, will be found a number of extracts from some of the laws written down in the days of Alfred. These laws, some of which have been quoted in one or two recent source-books, provide a rough table of "bots" or compensations for physical injuries sustained by assault. These may be worked out in a tariff by the class, and an exercise may be set on the reasons for the severity of some of the fines and on the justice or otherwise of the comparative "bots." Similar exercises may be set on other extracts from this very interesting work, notably on the subject of ordeals, which never fails to elicit eager commentaries from pupils. Nothing, perhaps, will give one a better idea of the low state of civilisation of the English of the early Middle Ages than the reading of the laws and regulations contained in this book.

Domesday Book provides us with a very large amount of material for source-work. It is, however, remarkable how few teachers avail themselves of the published translations of the various sections of this wonderful historical document. If the pages dealing with the particular locality, in which the school in question stands, be sought out and copied down, it will generally be found that the teacher is provided with quite a quantity of excellent material for interesting source-work. It is even worth while spending as much as a dozen lessons on the local survey, for besides stimulating interest in local history it will give an uncommonly good opportunity for an appreciation of some of the elementary facts relative to mediaeval society.

The life and death of Thomas Becket always forms an attractive subject for school-pupils. Here we have a very remote historical episode on which we happen to be particularly well informed. In the Rolls Series we shall find a number of large volumes containing a selection of "Materials for the History of Archbishop Becket," and, though the investigator will have to translate from the Latin, a number of quotations may be obtained to lay before classes. As a summary of the series of events which led to the murder, the chapter on Becket in Dean Stanley's "Memorials of Canterbury" forms an excellent guide. Incidentally it may be observed that the subject of Becket makes an admirable subject for a school historical play—and there are really very few such suitable incidents for dramatisation in the earlier period of the Middle Ages.

Magna Carta provides an almost endless series of exercises on a variety of constitutional points. The Church, scutage, justice, reliefs, wardship and marriage, the position of the Jews, the mediaeval parliament, merchants, London, in fact a vast number of subjects crops up here for discussion and illustration. One firm of publishers has recently undertaken a cheap reprint of Magna Carta, along with other important documents of English History, and, with the aid of the very full and scholarly monograph of McKechnie, it should be possible for the teacher to devise a great number of varying exercises on this subject. Hitherto the great majority of school text-books have slavishly followed the old traditional ideas of Magna Carta as a "bulwark of popular liberty"; it is really necessary that a senior class should have an opportunity of looking through the document and seeing what sort of a charter it really was. It will not do merely to tell our pupils that the old conception of Magna Carta was wrong, they must be made to see, by a perusal of the document itself, that it was wrong.

To break into the realms of poetic literature, the Prologue to Chaucer's "Canterbury Tales" provides some excellent and well-known portraits of typical characters of the later fourteenth century. These extracts, whether merely read to a class or used as the basis for exercises, may be profitably combined with other extracts from the more or less contemporary "Piers Plowman" of Langland. Later mediaeval poems of historical significance may be found in Wright's "Political Poems," and in the various publications of the Percy Society.

More's "Utopia" provides several extracts which can be used as bases for questions and exercises, particularly those passages relating to the development of sheep-farming and the decay of agriculture, while there is also a lengthy and instructive passage relative to the foreign policy of France and some of the other States of Western Europe. The enclosure question may also be illustrated by a well-known sermon of Latimer's, and other extracts from contemporary writers may be found in the pages of our various modern source-books. For the later Tudor period there is the excellent series of documents reprinted and edited by Prothero, continued into the Stuart period; and this is followed up by Gardiner's volume of documents relative to the reign of Charles I and the period of the Commonwealth.

"Cromwell's Letters and Speeches," edited by Carlyle, is another well-known collection of original sources, and may be frequently used for exercises of this description; these volumes are now published in a cheap series, whilst it is also now possible to obtain cheaply the Memoirs of Colonel Hutchinson and an abridgement of Bishop Burnet's "History of his Own Time." An almost endless list might be given of readily-obtainable volumes of original authority, while the various source-books and series of source-books ought most certainly to find a place in the school historical library. If access can be gained to Wellington's "Despatches" and Napoleon I's "Correspondence" much interesting material may be collected for school source-work.

The above illustrations will sufficiently indicate the variety of work that can be obtained from the use of sources; it must still always be borne in mind that such works must be kept in subordination to the main course of the syllabus.

It will be found that there are very few original authorities that can with any satisfaction be laid before a class of junior pupils. Even older ones are often perplexed by the obscurity of the legal language in which the more formal documents are couched and by the archaic or unfamiliar words that make their appearance in the records of earlier centuries. It will often be found advisable to simplify the language considerably and to strike out whole passages as being incomprehensible, dull or irrelevant, though care must be taken that this sort of informal editing does not alter the real meaning of the original words or help to convey a false impression; an indiscreet erasure of important passages and statements may alter the meaning of an extract as completely as Bismarck's blue pencil altered the meaning of the Ems telegram.

The same sort of occasional exercise on sources may be given in European history lessons. Here the original sources are harder to get at, though a start has already been made by the publication both of collections of documents relating to European history and of history books of European scope which contain extracts from contemporary writers. Within a year from the outbreak of the great European war in 1914 there appeared, for instance, a really excellent collection of documents relative to the European history of the last century, particularly to those events leading up to the outbreak of the great German war. There were, at the same time, the various White, Green and Orange Books of the Governments at war, providing excellent material for eliciting facts from records.

The foregoing suggestions relate entirely to original authorities, but there is another form of source-work that is extremely profitable. This is where the source of information used is not a first-hand authority, but the work of later writers and historians. This corresponds more closely to geographical map-work than does the exercise on original authorities. Let us take a few examples of this kind of thing. First there is the simpler form of exercise in which each pupil does the same work. Some well-known and easily accessible historical author is cited, and the pupils are given a fortnight or so to "get up" certain pages. As an example of such an exercise, Macaulay's essay on Clive may be chosen, or a selection from Cromwell's Letters, and a chapter of Froude's History. From the detailed narrative obtained here the pupils are asked either to write up an abstract, or to answer certain special questions on the work thus done. The disadvantage of this method is that when the available number of copies of the book in question is small, much time will have to be allowed in the preparation of the work for the volumes to be passed on from pupil to pupil.

Another and perhaps better method is to work on the following lines. The teacher makes a list of books relating to some particular historical subject—the Peninsular War, the loss of the American colonies, or the Revolution of 1689. Having done this, he allots passages in each of these volumes for the perusal of various members of the class, and then asks for a written *résumé* of the work each pupil has done. Several lessons can then be devoted to building up a historical summary of the episodes under investigation in concert with the class, using only the material supplied by the class.

A variation on the above method has been attempted at times with rather good results. Using the advantages offered by the proximity of a good public library, the older pupils may be told to look up the actual records of a debate in the House of Commons on some particular subject, the American War, the Reform Bill, the Corn Laws. The teacher will, of course, first make himself acquainted with the debate, and will allot parts to the pupils who are to look up materials; he will decide upon what speeches shall be prepared by the individual members of the class. Each pupil will then read up in the records the speech allotted to him, and, after making an abstract of notes, will prepare the same speech in miniature to be delivered from his notes. When the work has been all prepared, the "debate" is held;

the "members" rise one after the other in the historical order and a rough representation of the discussion in question is thus provided. Needless to say, the amount of trouble and work required for the preparation of a piece of work like this forbids its adoption more than once or twice in a school year.

There is yet another form of source-work which can be used in schools, which is at once the most pretentious, the most interesting, and the most time-absorbing. It can only be managed by those teachers who have the time and the patience to devote a part of their holidays or spare time to research work. This is nothing less than to build up a piece of history from all available historical authorities. Now the selection of a suitable topic will give rise to some perplexity, for we must take something about which there is neither a dearth nor a superfluity of records. For instance, if we chose the mission of St Augustine we could write down all our available materials in a very short space, while if we selected the Repeal of the Corn Laws or the siege of Sebastopol we should never be able to cope with a quarter of the sources at hand in our libraries. It is better to choose some definite episode, and not a continued series of episodes, rather the last year of Becket's life than the story of Henry II's relations with Becket, rather the battle of Marston Moor and its preceding military operations than the Civil War in 1644, rather the Gordon riots than the story of Catholic emancipation. The more spread out the subject chosen the more numerous and difficult to hit on will be our original authorities. When an episode has been selected, and one of some real historical importance should be taken, the teacher will take up the task of the historical investigator and will search out, copy, or translate all the relevant material he can lay hands on. The work is interesting, but consumes a great amount of time, and it would be well if any teacher who carries out a piece of work of this description would endeavour to secure the permanent benefit of his labours by the publication of the documents and extracts thus collected.

When a collection of this sort has been got together, it is best that the documents should be copied out for the hectograph or cyclostyle duplicator, so that each pupil of the class should be able to have a copy. From the sources thus presented the history of the episodes chosen can be built up at first-hand, and scope is given for a series of very interesting lessons in the methods of obtaining the truth about the past. Of course, these lessons must not occupy too much time, and the work done should also if possible fit in with the general programme of work set out in the syllabus adopted by the teacher.

We have thus briefly surveyed the possibilities contained in source-work, and it is evident that there is much to be done with this type of exercise. It will by no means, however, be considered advisable to adopt the extreme claims of the source-book enthusiasts and make our lessons nothing more than a long series of exercises on original authorities. Like many other special methods, it can be followed up *ad nauseam*, and a class will make far more progress on a balanced syllabus than on one which is too heavily weighted in one particular direction.

C. DRAMATISED HISTORY

It is remarkable to what a small extent history teachers have hitherto availed themselves of opportunities for using dramatic work as an aid to the teaching of their subject. In those schools in which dramatic work is attempted, it usually forms part of the training in literature or in the English language; but as a means of assisting and encouraging the study of history it has great possibilities.

There is a very general complaint among pupils that continuous application to the text-book and the exercise becomes dull. It is true that when the novelty of a new form of exercise or of a new text-book has worn off, the interest of some members of a class is bound to show signs of flagging. It will be said that a first-rate teacher will not allow this reaction to take place, that by his energies and his enthusiasm for his work he will keep his classes up to the mark all through the year, that a slackening of interest will be a token of partial failure, and so on. But the teacher need not altogether reproach himself if something of this sort makes itself apparent in his classes. A young teacher will often become quite mortified and embittered if he finds his enthusiastic efforts treated with scant respect and no gratitude by his less industrious pupils, but even the best of teachers has difficulties which he cannot get over but which he has to get round as best he can.

A really serious study of history is quite difficult for younger pupils, and even in the senior forms the more scientific aspect of the subject can only be tackled with an effort on the part of many boys and girls. It has been even argued that the real importance of historical matter varies in inverse proportion to the amount of superficial interest it evokes. It need only be remembered that our pupils nearly always prefer those pages of history which deal with the petty details of biographies, military actions and social habits and customs. An average class will be keenly inquisitive as to the personal peculiarities of Becket, Queen Elizabeth or Napoleon, without showing the remotest desire to enquire into their influence on the people of their country or the world in general. The reason why Crecy and Agincourt are better remembered than Halidon Hill and La Rochelle is that the former are usually given in our text-books in full and picturesque detail while the latter are at best dismissed in a couple of lines. The games and table manners of the Middle Ages are remembered long after the Guild System and the Curia Regis have faded from our pupils' minds.

This interest in the trivial can hardly be blamed; it is quite natural that the mind should be attracted mainly by those things which can be readily visualised, and that the broader conceptions of history should make comparatively little impression. We must utilise to the fullest extent the power of attraction possessed by the trivial. While keeping guard against introducing picturesque trivialities as an end in themselves, the teacher will do well to play upon them, especially with younger pupils, in order to lead up to and illustrate the more important factors in history.

At the present time there is little use made of dramatised history in our schools. The main reason for this is, perhaps, that lessons in which the pupils move about the room and act require a good deal more skilful organisation and management than lessons in which the class remains at the desks. It is not every teacher that can manage a lesson of this sort without allowing the additional freedom of movement and action to degenerate into disorder and breaches of discipline. Another reason is the extraordinary dearth of good historical plays suitable for boys and girls. The Shakespearian dramas, and those classic historical plays which appeal to adults, are usually too difficult in language and ideas for young pupils to understand, whilst the poetic dramatist rarely adheres very closely to historical accuracy. Though the great Duke of Marlborough is supposed to have got all the history he ever knew from Shakespeare's plays, they are not very satisfactory sources for the modern student.

The best historical school-plays are those which are more or less extemporised; the class discusses the possibility of acting a little scene to illustrate some point connected with its history lessons, it then discusses what characters are to be introduced, what they are to do, and what speeches are to be made. It is impossible to indicate in greater detail the way in which the crude idea of a bit of historical acting will develop into the finished article—a properly constructed scene or set of scenes acted by the class. As far as possible the scenes should be written by the pupils themselves, and if the teacher who wishes to experiment in this direction is in need of suggestions, he may be referred to Mr Caldwell Cook's "Play Way" and to the section on Dramatised History in "The New Teaching" edited by Professor John Adams.

Before leaving this topic, it may not be considered as exceeding the limits of our subject if we revert for a moment to the question of Shakespeare's "Histories" as suitable subjects for historical acting. Although the plays of Shakespeare are frequently acted by school pupils, and the staging of Shakespeare is rightly considered a mark of good taste in the school teacher, it may perhaps be doubted if the acting of these poetic works has as much really good effect on the pupils who act them and listen to them as on the "parents and guardians" who are sometimes fortunate enough to be admitted to witness the final productions. The genuine appreciation of the wonderful, unparalleled dramatic poetry of William Shakespeare can only come from a highly developed and imaginative mind. What steps can be taken to inculcate a taste for such works as his plays must be decided upon by those who have devoted their attention to specialising in the teaching of English literature, but for the purposes of a history course it must be said that Shakespeare's plays cannot be used effectively except in the very highest forms. The difficulty of the phraseology, the obsolete and rare words, the poetic digressions and metaphorical allusions of the Shakespearian play are altogether above the average pupil of middle and lower forms, and it is a mistake to try and force him to grapple with these things. Such an effort may perhaps be called for in the literature class, where the works of our great writers are being dealt with for their own sakes, but in the history class, where the play is used as a means to an end, there are few passages that can be quoted at length without such copious explanation and comment as will lead us to outrun the time at our disposal. And when we come to consider the advisability, not merely of quoting them, but of acting them, the same remarks apply with even greater force. To attempt to simplify or alter their language would, of course, be a piece of literary vandalism which could not be tolerated for a moment.

The possibilities which lie behind the adoption of some attempts at the dramatisation of history have now been briefly indicated. The work demands the utmost attention of the teacher, and will prove one more source of the invasion of his time. If it cannot be done with real enthusiasm and energy on the part of the teacher, it had best not be done at all. But for those whose bent lies somewhat in the direction of the drama, it will prove one of the most interesting and pleasant parts of the history course, and we shall have the satisfaction of knowing that, whilst giving rise to a very considerable amount of pleasure to all who are concerned in the work, we shall also be most decidedly contributing to the consolidation of the historical knowledge of our pupils, and to the stimulation and development of a further interest in history.

In concluding this chapter it may be as well to note that there are quite a number of good historical plays going the round of British theatres. Some of these plays are of long standing, others are new, and there will doubtless be some good new ones brought out each year. The teacher's all-devouring intelligence department should take cognisance of these, and, when the school happens to lie within easy reach of the theatre, arrangements can usually be made with the manager for the admission of a party of pupils at reduced rates, an opportunity which should be used by the teacher and by as many of the pupils as can afford the necessary expense.

D. LOCAL HISTORY

It has been mentioned that it is desirable to include in a school course a certain number of lessons on local history, lessons which are fittingly introduced into the syllabus for middle forms. Now local history may be utilised in several ways. In the first place we can attempt to trace the development of the particular city, town or county in which we happen to find our school situated, outlining its progress as a unit of local government. Secondly we can find out what incidents of more national importance have taken place in the neighbourhood and devote some time to the description of them. Thirdly we can illustrate our larger national history by references to what actually or putatively happened in one particular district. All three of these methods are useful from the point of view of the teacher.

There will naturally be a very great difference in the opportunities for the study of local history in different parts of the country. If a school is situated in an old city or town rich in historical incidents and records, such a place as London, Canterbury, York, Norwich, Bristol or Exeter, there will be a plenitude of materials on which to draw for lessons; if on the other hand the school is situated in a small town of little historical importance, or in the middle of some rural district, there will be a dearth of such materials. There are some places which may be said to have virtually no local history. Again, there are some parts of the Kingdom which, owing to their remoteness from the centres of agricultural, industrial and commercial activity have been little affected by the great upheavals of history and have witnessed no great national events in their immediate neighbourhood. In cases of this sort we shall have to fall back almost entirely on the third method, for no matter where our school is situated, it will be found to have been in some degree affected by those greater movements which pervaded the whole nation, movements like the Reformation and the Civil War, the Industrial Revolution or the Agricultural Revolution.

There is a variety of material to be found in libraries for the study of local history. There is usually a fair number of books on the subject, some old and some new. For some counties there is the Victoria County History. Almost every shire in England has its collection of topographical and historical volumes. Then there will be more detailed books on particular cities and towns. It will nearly always be found that there exist maps of the district in past times; some towns and counties are particularly rich in this respect. An examination of the catalogues of local libraries supplemented by consultation with the librarians will often bring to light much useful material. There is also, for most parts of England, Domesday Book, which should certainly not be neglected.

A word may be said as to the use of local guide-books. These are of very varying standards of value; a few have been compiled with genuine attention to historical authenticity, but by far the larger number bear the marks of having been hastily and carelessly written up for the sole purpose of providing something superficially interesting for the ordinary tourist irrespective of authenticity or accuracy. For the purposes of school work, the popular local guide-book may very well be taken as a starting-point, provided that the teacher takes care to verify its statements and correct its errors.

From the authorities mentioned above it will be possible for the teacher to prepare a series of lessons on local history. If the school is situated in a town, the pupils should know how that town has grown, or in a few cases shrunk, to what date the various quarters of the town can be assigned, the age and history of the celebrated buildings, the history of the organisation for local government, the names and careers of the local celebrities. In connection with this last subject, there is another field for work opened up. In a junior biographical course room should most certainly be found for the lives of men and women of the locality who have distinguished themselves in national history, and also for the lives of others who have by their actions brought fame to the particular locality in which the pupils reside.

Great national events which have taken place in our own district should be treated in some detail, and perhaps may be studied on the actual ground on which they took place. Thus the pupils of schools in and near the city of York should be made acquainted with as many details as possible of the battles of Stamford Bridge, Towton and Marston Moor; the pupils of schools in Bristol should learn particularly about the setting forth of John Cabot, of the siege of 1643, and of the Reform Bill riots.

Thirdly there is the presumptive or authentic local history which can be deduced from the great movements of the national history. Even if there is a scarcity of material for other sorts of local history, even if there are no materials available at all, it should still be possible to give quite a long series of lessons of this sort. Every part of southern Britain must have felt the presence of the Romans, most of the English counties must have seen severe fighting when the Jutes, Angles and Saxons came here. Again, the preaching of the Christian missionaries must have been heard in every district, and the ravages of the Northmen too must have been felt almost everywhere. All these events can be made to fit in with a course of local history, and if authentic local facts can be obtained to illustrate these movements, so much the better.

The feudal organisation presents the next means of illustrating local developments; we can trace the probable effects of feudalism in our own locality. Then there are the Crusades, which probably drew at least one or two volunteers from the neighbourhood, while it may be that we are situated on an estate belonging once to some great baron who rebelled against his royal suzerain. The Livery system probably had its effect locally, and the Wars of the Roses may usually be found to affect the neighbourhood in some way or other. Coming to more modern times, we have the various changes of the Reformation, and later on the great struggle between Anglican and Puritan. The Agricultural Revolution and the Industrial Revolution, the agitation for Democracy and the reform of local government will also be found to affect every part of the realm.

Some places are fortunate enough to possess in their neighbourhood a castle or an abbey either in a good state of preservation or in ruins. These survivals from the past should be utilised to the utmost. If possible, maps should be drawn to illustrate the arrangement of the buildings at the time they enjoyed their palmiest days; models of them may even be constructed. The monastery, with its chapel and dining-hall, its buttery and bakery, its dormitories and *scriptorium*, may be made to live again; the same may be done with the castle; keep, inner ward, outer ward, flanking towers, moat, portcullis and drawbridge may be reconstructed from the surviving remains.

The manner in which the castle or the religious house affected the life of the surrounding district may also be indicated.

Of course those schools which are situated in the metropolis enjoy an advantage in respect to local history higher than those of any other place. Yet there is a special problem connected with the history of London which only presents itself elsewhere when the town in which a school is situated is of very large size indeed. As there are some thousands of teachers who are giving instruction in history in London, it may be worth while to turn for a moment to consider the problem in relation to this great city.

London is so vast a place as to suggest rather a collection of towns than a single city. It spreads for miles in every direction around the little city of the Middle Ages. People living at one extremity of it are often in total ignorance of the quarters at the other end, and even of the central districts too. A century ago, the local history of places like Hampstead, Tottenham, Bow, Woolwich, Sydenham, Wandsworth, Hammersmith and Paddington would have been quite distinct from the local history of London, for London was a more or less remote city whilst these places were country villages or towns. But at the present day these places all form part, if not of the County of London, at least of what we term Greater London, and their inhabitants would not dream of calling themselves by any other local name than Londoners. As Londoners they naturally claim the history of London as that of their own homes. It will therefore be advisable and almost necessary to teach the history of the City of London to pupils in districts which are in many cases some miles away from the old municipal boundaries, and to pupils who have in many cases never been to the City or to Westminster at all. Only a few years ago, at an elementary school in the north of the Borough of Lambeth, the pupils were given a series of questions on their personal migrations. It was found that more than a score had never crossed over to the north side of the Thames, and that three had never even seen that river, though it flowed within four hundred yards of the school in question.

Our difficulties in a case like this are very great. In the first place it is necessary to make our pupils acquainted with the topography of the central parts of London as they stand at the present day. It will be worth while to set up a little correlation between the history and the geography classes in this respect. Geography teachers do frequently overlook the claims of local topography, largely perhaps because the modern development of scientific geography teaching has placed mere topographical description at a discount. If the pupil could get some topographical knowledge of central London in his geography lessons it would be a great help to the study of local history as well as an advantage for its own sake. Of course maps will be frequently drawn to illustrate the growth of the city at various periods, and the leading thoroughfares may be marked on these maps. Also, when a school visit is made to any building or place of interest or to any central theatre, care must be taken to point out the main streets through which the class may happen to go.

Thus for the London teacher local history has a double significance, the history of the parish or the borough and the history of the City and of central London. The latter, of course, provides an endless theme for lessons, and may frequently be illustrated by maps, pictures and school visits to places of historical interest in the central districts of the metropolis.

There is another aspect of local history that may be remarked. This is the study of street-names; often a most enlightening study. A large percentage of our town street-names have an historical significance. In the old central parts of an historical borough they indicate in many cases the topographical features of the mediaeval town. In London we have Cheapside, the Old Bailey, the Poultry, Fleet Street, the Strand, Northumberland Avenue and Bankside as examples; in Leeds we have the Briggate, Kirkgate Marsh, and the Calls; in Nottingham we have Greyfriars Gate, Fletcher Gate, Chapel Bar and Lean Side; in Edinburgh we have the Canongate, the Lawn Market, and Candlemaker Row. There is another large section of street-names that commemorates local worthies and national celebrities, while the names of modern battles and sieges like Waterloo, Alma, Sebastopol and Ladysmith usually indicate the period at which the streets so named were built.

In connection with local history we may deal with the subject of school visits. It is good to arrange an occasional visit to some place of historical importance, a castle, church, abbey or museum. The number of pupils under the direction of a single teacher should not be too large, one class at a time will usually be found enough. These school visits, like everything else connected with teaching, require considerable and careful preparation. It is not enough to take the class round the run of sights and extemporise remarks on them. The teacher should first make the excursion himself and arrange exactly what things are going to be seen, find out all he can about them, and make up his mind what he will say about them. Some teachers will prefer to reserve all remarks of this sort until the actual excursion or visit, but it will appear to some more satisfactory to prepare a short series of notes beforehand and to let the class have these and discuss them before the visit is made. Sometimes, with an older class it may even seem good to allow individual pupils to attempt the talking and explaining, while the teacher merely corrects and adds and summarises. Again, the work should not end with the visit; a composition or summary of what has been seen should most certainly form the usual sequel of a school visit. Otherwise the impression made will be somewhat unsubstantial and fleeting. Finally it may be pointed out that on no account should an historical excursion be looked on as a mere "outing" for purposes of amusement, especially if it is carried out in school hours; it must be considered by both teacher and pupils as a regular working lesson, although more or less *in partibus*.

The study of local history is of real importance, and should most certainly find some space, however small, in the school history syllabus. For besides bringing home to the pupil in vivid fashion the various historical movements which have affected the nation, it lends an air of interest and romance to otherwise dull and colourless local surroundings, and it helps to bring home to the pupil, by everyday contact with historical scenes, names and buildings, the sense of the development which his country has undergone, and removes his thoughts from time to time away from the present to the contemplation of ages that are passed.

E. EUROPEAN AND GENERAL HISTORY

If local history may be considered a fitting accompaniment to the middle-form course of English history, European and general history will be most conveniently taught in conjunction with the more scientific course of the upper forms. It has already been pointed out how essential it is that some lessons on European history should be introduced into the school course and also that such lessons should be kept as far as possible separate from the English history lessons. Now the question that will immediately arise is, How much general history shall we teach? The vastness of the subject has in fact terrified many teachers into refusing to touch it at all; it has been relegated to the sphere of the university, or left to private reading, or even ignored altogether. But the chief point to remember is that without some reference to the main outlines of European development our own history remains incomplete and unbalanced; nobody would for one moment suggest that our geography lessons should be limited to the study of the British Isles, or even of the Empire; without some knowledge of the greater physical features of the globe our own local geography would be equally incomplete and unbalanced. It is, then, absurd to bury our heads in the sand of insular exclusiveness and shun a conflict with the question of teaching European history.

But the great question of time is undoubtedly one which affects our position in regard to European history. In a recent conference of history teachers, when the various specialists in different branches of our subject rose and delivered their intensely interesting suggestions for improving this and that branch of the teaching of history, there was always an undercurrent of impatience among the audience at the apparently endless demands that were being made in lecture after lecture on the time at the disposal of the average instructor. Now this feeling arose from the fact that the great majority of the members were all-round teachers of history while many of the lecturers were enthusiasts in some particular branch of history teaching. It is natural that an enthusiast should like to push the claims of his particular speciality to the utmost extent possible, but many of the audience failed to make this allowance when they listened to the speakers' suggestions. The duty of the history teacher is to hear and consider all suggestions, and after making the due allowances it will be found possible and indeed advantageous to introduce some element of all the different types of historical study into our course.

In European history this problem of time is certainly a most pressing one. For we shall certainly not be able to devote more than a small number of lessons to the subject, perhaps half a dozen or so during the term. There is a call, therefore, for a very careful selection of material, so as to make sure that we get the really essential and do not waste time over minor topics. It has already been indicated how we should proceed in this respect, how local and petty matters must be subordinated to broad views and general outlines, how the national histories of the various States are to be utilised only as illustrating broad and extensive movements.

A very brief survey of the great movements of European history may perhaps give some suggestion of the method most suitable for application. The extent of the

Roman Empire, its system of centralised government and the causes of its overthrow should certainly be known. Then there comes the reconstruction of western Europe under the Barbarian Kings. The origin and spread of Mohammedanism come next, and we must trace the advent of the wave of Saracen conquest into Europe, turned back by Leo the Isaurian at Constantinople, but sweeping over the Spanish peninsula into the plains of Gaul. The rise and the supremacy of the Franks in western Europe must next be outlined, the conflict of Eastern and Western civilisation on the plains of Tours, and the forcing of the Orientals back over the Pyrenees, Then comes Charlemagne with the revived Roman Empire of the West, which splits asunder under the influence of its own inherent weaknesses and the pressure of the Northmen from outside. This naturally leads up to the organisation of the feudal method of self-defence, aided by those eastern and southern counterparts of the Northmen, the Magyars and the Saracen pirates. This brings us to the period when western Europe settled down as a feudally-organised civilisation, still divided into large and more or less national units, but effectively dissected into a vast conglomeration of petty lordships and republics.

Behind this reticulated collection of mediaeval feudal lordships looms the fading shadow of Imperial Rome. Its claims are represented by two powers, the secular arm of the Holy Roman Emperor of the German Nation and the Supreme Pontiff of the Roman Church. The internecine and suicidal strife between the successor of Caesar and the successor of St Peter must be briefly explained, while our attention is then drawn off westwards to the achievement of national unity by France and Spain under the influence of foreign warfare, in the first case with the English, in the second case with the Moors. Then comes the invasion of the

Turks, and the collapse of all that was left of the old Roman Empire of the East. The Renaissance and the age of discovery can now be briefly dealt with, and this naturally leads on to the Reformation and its extension. The results of the Reformation may be outlined in their relation to France, Spain, Germany, Holland, and other countries; this involves brief and cursory glances at the Huguenot persecution, the Inquisition, the Thirty Years' War, and the establishment of the independent United Provinces of the Netherlands.

The development of international politics next demands our attention. First we must sketch the greatness of the power of Spain under Philip II, the causes of its rise and the causes of its fall. The greatness of Spain gives place to the greatness of France, as we trace the rise of the latter Power from Henry IV to Richelieu, from Richelieu to Mazarin, from Mazarin to Louis XIV. The theory and practice of the Balance of Power can here be explained and illustrated. The eighteenth century brings us to the rise of the two new eastern Powers, Prussia and Russia. Then come the Industrial Revolution, the French Revolution, and the great European war against regenerated Republican France. When we have briefly sketched the characteristics and the results of the Revolutionary and Napoleonic wars, we can turn aside to review the map of Europe as settled by the Treaty of Vienna in 1815. Here we embark upon the most recent period of European history. As already indicated, the best method of dealing with this period is to take in turn the three great series of movements which have proved to be the most important and determining factors in the development of the Continent during the past century—democracy, nationalism and international rivalry.

We have thus scantily indicated those great leading

movements of the history of Europe which ought to form the basis of our lessons on the subject. The course may, if the general plan indicated in the chapter on the syllabus be followed, be spread out over three, or if necessary over four years of study.

In planning our lessons, we should never lose sight of the main threads of history or be led aside into petty detail of no illustrative importance. One or two examples of suitable lessons in European history may be given. The subjects we will choose as examples are the Empire and the Papacy, the Thirty Years' War, and the conquests of Napoleon. It will be seen that in each case the subject has to be organised as a harmonious whole before presentation to the class. In dealing with the struggle of the Empire and the Papacy we must first outline the position and claims of the two forces. The Empire represents the traditional sway of the Caesar, the secular power of the Roman Empire. The Church inherits the power of Rome in the spiritual sphere, and the Pope increases his influence by utilising the Scriptures and the Christian Fathers to show the necessity of all Christians submitting to the overlordship of the successor of St Peter. When Charlemagne took the crown from the hands of Leo III, he inaugurated a union of Empire and Papacy in which the former was the dominant partner. For two centuries or more this arrangement holds together, but the pretensions of the Papacy are gradually growing. Hildebrand develops the doctrine of papal supremacy; he equips the Church of Rome with a magnificent centralised organisation, and claims the lordship of all princes. There followed a great struggle between the Empire and the Papacy, but there were underlying forces which gave force and variety to the struggle. In one way this struggle was a conflict between Germans and Italians, though there are certain exceptions to be made. Many German feudal barons took the side of the Pope to serve their own purposes, while many Italian nobles, afraid of the consequences of an over-mighty Papacy so near their own estates, joined the Emperor's party. The struggle need not be outlined in any detail. Henry IV, Frederick Barbarossa, Frederick II, may be mentioned as leading champions of the Imperial party; Hildebrand, Alexander III, and Innocent III as the chief figures on the other side. The humiliation of Canossa should certainly be introduced, as also the scheme for uniting Naples with Germany. Finally we should attempt to summarise the causes of the ultimate papal triumph, the exhaustion of the military resources of Imperial and feudal Germany, the successful intrigues and rebellions of the German barons, the defensive patriotism of the Italians, the elastic invincibility of the Roman Catholic dogmas.

Taking another example, we may outline the treatment to be recommended in the case of the Thirty Years' War. This was a religious war between the Catholics and Protestants of Germany; it passed through four phases, in which the dominant party of the Catholics, led by Austria, overcame the Protestants and their foreign allies. The first phase is purely German, and is soon settled by the conquest of Bohemia, the leading Protestant State, and the victories of the Catholic troops. The second phase begins with the entrance upon the scene of King Christian of Denmark as the ally of the defeated Protestants, and ends in a second great Catholic victory. The third phase sees Gustavus Adolphus of Sweden enter the lists as Protestant champion, but after several victories he is killed at the battle of Lützen and the Swedes are thenceforward gradually driven out of Germany. The fourth phase brings on the stage the sinister figure of Cardinal Richelieu, a Catholic and a persecutor of Protestants at home, but abroad the ally of the Protestants who are going to serve French national interests. The Catholics cannot beat the powerful forces of the French monarchy, and the Peace of Westphalia is arranged, by which the Protestants keep most of their land and their religious independence, while Richelieu's policy secures Alsace for France.

The subject of Napoleon's foreign conquests will provide us with a third example. Having described how Napoleon organised France under a strong centralised despotism with himself as the keystone of the edifice, we proceed to the expansion of his sphere of influence beyond the borders of France. First we may take the districts actually annexed to the Empire itself. The Directory had secured Belgium and the Rhine frontier; he proceeded to conquer still further provinces. There is Holland, first made a dependent republic, then a kingdom for Louis, finally absorbed into the Empire. There is the north-western district of Germany annexed in order more effectively to prevent the entrance of British goods to the Continent. There is the great slice of north-west Italy, and there is the north-east province of Spain. Then we have the outlying Illyrian provinces east of the Adriatic. We can next go on to indicate the subject States, Jerome's Westphalian kingdom, Murat's Neapolitan kingdom, Joseph's Spanish kingdom and the Emperor's own kingdom of Italy, with the Swiss Confederacy, the Grand-Duchy of Warsaw and the Confederation of the Rhine. Then we take Prussia, garrisoned by French troops and bound hand and foot to the French alliance, and Austria, less under Napoleon's heel but still part of the great Napoleonic hegemony, Sweden ruled by a Napoleonic Marshal as Crown-Prince, Denmark friendly and Portugal in process of conquest. Finally we have Russia, still free but agreeing to arrange her commerce to suit the convenience of the French Emperor. There is no need to trace the steps by which these conquests were made. The names of a few leading battles like Austerlitz and Wagram should be given in a brief sketch of Napoleon's talents as a general, but for a school-course further detail is unnecessary.

Wherever possible the teacher should elicit comparisons between the events abroad and similar or corresponding events at home. Thus the Roman Empire may be illustrated from the province of Britain, the Anglo-Saxon invasion can be compared with the contemporary barbarian invasions on the Continent, and the conflict of Popes and Emperors quoted in reference to the conflicts of Henry I and Henry II with Anselm and Becket. Similarly, in a later period, we can compare the Thirty Years' War with our own religious Civil War, the democratic movements of the continental states with our own democratic movements, and the nationalist question in Austria-Hungary or Poland with the nationalist question in Ireland.

In the teaching of European history frequent use should be made of the map. It will take a long time for the pupil to get accustomed to the look of the old maps of the Continent, and therefore map-exercises should be fairly frequent. The following is a selection of maps, most of which should be drawn by the pupils: The Roman Empire, the Barbarian Kingdoms, Europe in 800 A.D., Europe in 1500, Europe in 1789, Europe in 1812 and Europe in 1815. Some knowledge of the political configuration of the Continent at these periods should certainly be obtained. Other maps, such as one of Italy to illustrate the Union, or one of the Ottoman Empire and its subject races, will suggest themselves as suitable subjects for exercises.

We must turn for a moment to the rather difficult question of how far we ought to widen the European course to include the history of the other continents. In modern times the non-European peoples have had little influence upon our own and the European peoples, except inasmuch as they have offered a tempting opportunity for aggressive colonial expansion. Of most of them it is enough to indicate in a few words the general state of civilisation they had reached when they came into contact with the white race. The colonial expansion of the European Powers should certainly be briefly outlined, but as the other races of the modern world have influenced us so slightly, it is hardly worth while attempting to enter into their rather uninspiring history. One exception deserves special mention. The rise of modern Japan merits its inclusion in the history course, as a striking example of the influence of our own civilisation on the civilisation of a distant and different race, and as showing the possibilities which lie before the non-European States if they choose to imitate Western methods. Forty years ago Japan was considered by the English as a curious and absurd oriental kingdom fit only to be the subject of a comic opera; at the present time Japan holds her head high among the nations, and the British have been proud to hail her as an ally.

But there is another collection of communities which demand attention, the white communities that have broken off their political allegiance to the European States. We teach the history of the English colonies on the Atlantic coast of America down to the point when they secured their independence at the Treaty of Versailles. But should we go on to indicate the lines of development pursued by the United States after that event? It seems that we should have omitted something of importance if we neglected to give two or three lessons to the subject of the United States and their problems. Again, there exist in America more than a dozen independent republics, some of them of very considerable size, ruled by the Spanish and Portuguese peoples. These republics have risen in some cases to a position of importance in the world, and it gives rather a false balance to modern history if we omit all reference whatever to these new States. Mexico, Brazil and Argentina are too big to be neglected, and when we come to our recent period in European history, time can certainly be found for one lesson, or perhaps for two, in which we can indicate their historical existence and their chief political characteristics.

A further question remains. History goes back to extremely early times, and general history includes the story of some great nations of remote antiquity. Are we to attempt to go back into these early times and teach our pupils the history of the great civilisations of antiquity? They are important even from the present-day point of view, for we get our days of the week, our alphabet and many of our literary and artistic ideas from these early civilisations. But here at least we must call a halt. A few words on the subject of the older civilisations may be introduced when we speak of the Roman Empire, but the details of their institutions and their works must be left out altogether. Their history does not run, like mediaeval and modern European history, parallel with our own English history; their influence on us at the present day is largely indirect and remote, and they are not to be considered as absolutely essential to the understanding of the history of our own country. Greek and Roman history may perhaps be worked in as part of the classical course, but we cannot find a place for ancient history in the ordinary school history course.

F. RECENT HISTORY

THERE have occasionally been discussions on the question how far it is possible and desirable to teach in schools the history of the last few decades. This period is often neglected in the school history course, perhaps largely because of the difficulties which lie in the way of teaching it in a satisfactory manner. Why is it that the Victorian era is so much neglected in history teaching? Perhaps the first reason that will enter the mind is that the period is by no means so attractive to young pupils as are the more remote ages. At a first glance the Victorian era appears an age of frock-coats, parliamentary debates, social problems and party politics; and however interesting these matters may be to the adult student, it can hardly be expected to appeal to the young pupil in quite the same way as the violent and bloodthirsty Middle Ages or the adventurous days of Queen Elizabeth, or even the age of Wellington's redcoats and the three-bottle school of statesmen of Pitt's day.

But when we come to consider the question, is it really true that the recent period is as devoid of action and colour as is usually taken for granted? There is plenty of picturesque and stirring detail to be found in the history of the Indian Mutiny and the Crimean War. And in more recent times still the development of our distant colonies, the details of the Boer war, the Fenian agitation and other topics can be made as attractive as any episodes in our history. As a matter of fact, most of our text-books concentrate far too much on the warlike activities of the Middle Ages and far too much on the constitutional measures of the modern period; the mediaeval constitution and the building up of our colonial empire are both capable of far more systematic and thorough treatment than they usually receive either in the books or in class.

In any question relating to the teaching of recent history the "bias" difficulty inevitably springs up. There have been long discussions as to how far partiality is to be condoned in a teacher of history. There are some who hold that partiality cannot be avoided, a few who hold that it ought not to be avoided, and others who recommend and demand the strictest impartiality in the teacher.

As a matter of fact, no real grasp of history can be obtained unless the student makes his enquiries in a spirit of impartiality. The man who goes to history to find proofs of political or religious theories, which he has already accepted, runs the danger of altogether failing to understand the events and movements about which he reads. Apart from the promptings of conscience, which will probably influence most of those who are not violent partisans, the desire to approach their subject in a level-headed scientific manner ought to prevent the history specialist from erring in this respect. Where there are complaints of bias in school history teaching, it will usually be found that it is the teacher of general subjects, and not the specialist, who turns the history lesson into an opportunity for preaching his own political or religious theories.

The conscientious and scientific history teacher will attempt to do justice to both sides of the questions at issue in recent history, and so to deal with controversial topics that the strong points on either side are brought into prominence. There are always reasons to be found for and against any policy; where parties differ it is because each lays different degrees of emphasis upon the various factors to be considered in the question at issue. The historian has to point out what these factors were and which factors received special emphasis in the ideas of each political or religious party. The main duty of the historian is to show how human society has developed through the ages, not to set himself up as a moral critic of the rights and wrongs of political factions and religious sects—far less of rival statesmen and politicians.

There is, however, a great field of recent history that does not lay itself open to any great extent to party treatment. Though the "Opposition" of the day has had much to say about the abominable way the Government of the day has conducted the wars, one can deal with most of our foreign and colonial contests with outside enemies during the last century with comparative detachment and impartiality; or, if there is any partiality, it will probably be of a patriotic sort, and that is not so harmful. Though Imperialism and Little Englandism have in the past had some very nasty conflicts, the wonderful development of our Empire should provide a theme on which much useful information can be given without bias. This part of English history—the development of our oversea dominions during the last century—has been one of the most neglected of the chapters of history taught in our schools, though it is surely of enormous importance. Few school pupils have been told of the foundation of Rhodesia, Louís Riel's rebellion, the Klondyke gold rush, the convict disputes in Australia, the Eureka stockade, the Maori wars, how Perim was occupied, and a hundred other important and really interesting topics of colonial history.

As a matter of fact, it is really more important that a pupil should master some knowledge about the last century than that he should know about the earlier ages. Of course, the more history he can learn the better, if it is of the right quality; but if the history of the last two generations is to be neglected while the Hundred Years' War and the career of Cromwell are to be studied in detail, then something is decidedly wrong. Teachers should not forget to allot a sufficiency of time in the syllabus to the most recent decades of history, and, in the hands of thoughtful and tactful men and women, there should be no serious difficulty either in avoiding political partiality or in investing the subject with a living interest.

It may, perhaps, here be pointed out that a number of really good and useful exercises can be set on points of recent history. Again a few examples may be given. A class may be provided with a summary showing the chief features of the three Home Rule Bills of 1886, 1893 and 1912. The class may then be asked to compare the three and to point out in what particulars the three bills differ. Again, statistics of the number of Catholics and Protestants in the different counties of Ireland may be given, and a map of Ireland drawn to show, by shading, which counties are mainly under the influence of the former, and which of the latter. In the next lesson the class may make a similar map showing political representation, Unionist and Nationalist, and a comparison of the two maps may follow. The King's Speech on the opening of a parliamentary session may be read from the newspaper, and a series of questions given on references in the speech. The Budget revenues may be written on the blackboard and questions set; perhaps the figures and items may be compared with those of an eighteenth century Budget. An abbreviation of some of Sir John French's despatches may be read to a class—perhaps those relating to the retreat from Mons in 1914—a map can be made by each pupil to show the route pursued. Two war despatches, "German official" and "Russian official," may be read, describing some particularly important operations in the Great European War, with the aid of a sketch-map on the blackboard. They may be compared, the chief points taken as notes, and an account of what happened written up from a comparison of the two. The navy lists of the Powers of Europe in a given year may be compared, and a diagram can be drawn showing the comparative number of battleships or submarines. These are merely examples of many exercises that will suggest themselves to the teacher.

Though we may not perhaps wish to encourage our schoolboys and schoolgirls to become newspaper-readers, it is certainly necessary to prepare them for the time when they will become such, and if we do not equip them in some measure with the mental background that will enable them to understand and to appreciate the columns devoted to domestic and foreign political intelligence, they will be inclined, when they begin to read newspapers, to regard them as interesting only for the sports results and for the police-court column. Foreign political intelligence has always occupied a fair share of space in the columns of our daily press; it obtained a special interest and even a predominance with the outbreak of the Great European War. It should be part of the duty of the history course to provide for this very practical aim, to train British citizens to make intelligent use of the material laid before them daily by the British Press. History teachers would be doing a good service to their senior pupils if they were to indicate the fact that important aid towards an understanding of contemporary history may be obtained from a perusal of the big Reviews. Many, perhaps most of our pupils leave the secondary schools without any idea of what sort of matter is contained in such volumes as the *Nineteenth Century*, *Blackwood's*, and *The Round Table*.

Ill-informed as the British daily papers often are on foreign political affairs, it is essential that a student should have the means of consulting the more accurate and balanced articles of the reviews as a corrective to the superficial and often misguided opinion of "our special correspondent" in the foreign capital. The occasional reading of a French or German newspaper or review, too, is surprisingly illuminating to those conversant with the foreign language.

When, at the outbreak of war in 1914, many teachers found themselves planning and giving lessons on the European situation and its causes, it was often borne in upon their minds in a striking manner how remarkably ignorant they had allowed their senior pupils to remain in matters connected with the great factors of recent world-history. To the average school pupil Germany was a country whose history, so far as it was known at all, terminated with the production of Blücher as a *deus ex machina* on the field of Waterloo. Even the Franco-German war was unknown to many of our pupils. The Russians were a race whom we had fought at Balaclava and Inkerman, and who wanted to take India away from us; while Japan had no history at all. Vague traditions of great deeds and events, picked up from the conversations of parents and other adults, suggested that there had been a battle of Sedan, an Emperor Napoleon III, an Armenian massacre, some riots and murders in Russia, an American Civil War, and a siege of Port Arthur. Our school course of instruction in history should be planned so as to include some means of giving to these airy nothings a local habitation and a name.

The last half-century, important though it is for the present generation, is still sadly neglected in our schools, and one reason for this is to be found in the fact that teachers often spend so much time over the earlier part of the year's syllabus that there is no time to complete it. We should not forget the injunction: *Respice finem.* We should keep our eye on the calendar, and if we find that we are slipping behind in our scheme of lessons, we should speed things up (even at the expense of the earlier decades) in order that we may have full time to deal with the later. The school pupils of past generations were generally like Gilbert's Major-General, whose knowledge, while embracing every detail of Caractacus' uniform, did not extend beyond the beginning of the nineteenth century. But with a proper care for the interests of recent history, we may hope to educate boys and girls who will regard history, not as the record of a dead past, but as a continuous chain whose newest links we ourselves are helping to forge.

II. HISTORY AND ALLIED STUDIES

It was formerly the custom for framers of the school curriculum to keep the various subjects apart as much as possible. There was to be no conscious co-operation between the teacher of history and the teachers of geography, English and other subjects. During the last dozen years, however, an opposite tendency has made itself manifest, and the educational world has been almost satiated with schemes of correlation. One set of extremists, indeed, goes so far as to lay down the principle that, all learning being one, the various lessons of the school, at least of the elementary school, should receive no separate names on the syllabus, each being considered part and parcel of a general course of instruction in elementary knowledge.

Now history, being so wide and diverse a subject, has many points of contact with other subjects, for since it is the science of human development and progress it must necessarily concern itself with almost all branches of knowledge. It brings us into contact with geography, with literature and language, with science, with engineering, with art, and to a certain extent with astronomy, with mathematics and with physiology. These subjects are connected with history in two distinct ways. Firstly, we can take, in all these cases, the history of the subject in its development as a science or as a study, Thus we have the history of the English language, the history of mechanical invention, the history of mathematical research. Secondly, each of these subjects at times is found to exert some sort of influence on the development of mankind.

A few examples of this may be quoted. The poems of Langland and Chaucer undoubtedly exerted some influence on public opinion in the later fourteenth century. The discoveries of Kepler and Galileo had not a little to do with the promotion of distant exploration and with the spread of the Protestant Reformation. The physical features of Great Britain vastly affected the course taken by the Anglo-Saxon conquest. The discoveries of Watt and Stephenson and Fulton were the mainspring of the Industrial Revolution. The climate of Russia was the decisive factor in Napoleon's Moscow campaign.

We must devote some space to the discussion of the question how we can best establish the relations of these varied subjects with history. Are we to let them remain separate and disconnected, leaving it to the common intelligence of the pupil to trace the connecting links between them, or are we to work consciously to the end of establishing a connection? It will not be denied that there is much exercise for the mind provided in frequent cross-reference from work in one subject to work in another. It will add, too, to the interest felt in one subject if it can be shown to have some bearing on another. There is a danger in the system of watertight compartments—the danger that pupils will begin to look upon school subjects as mere learned sciences and studies, unconnected with human life and revolving in little orbits of their own. If we wish to make the importance of a knowledge of history impress itself on the minds of our boys and girls, we must not only constantly refer past developments and events to those of our own day, but also show on every possible occasion the bearing of history on other subjects. The same applies to these other subjects as well.

As for the history of the development of each particular

science, it will probably be best if the instructors in each subject are left to provide the necessary information. Thus the chemistry teacher will teach the development of chemical research, the mathematical teacher will deal with the great mathematicians of history, and the English teacher will trace the history of language, metre and style. But there is much scope for correlation of the other type. History teachers will find very frequent cause to bring in references to other subjects, and other teachers will find many occasions on which it will be useful and necessary to illustrate their lessons by historical allusions.

Now this form of mutual assistance requires very careful organising, and is a far more difficult matter than may appear at first. The history teacher, were he on the spot, would know the exact moments when historical information might be given during lessons on other subjects, and the exact information necessary on each occasion. In most elementary schools, and in those other schools where one teacher takes several subjects, this difficulty does not usually arise. But in any school which has adopted the specialist system, progress in this respect is far more difficult, for in most cases the specialist instructor is so wrapped up in his own subject that he rarely inclines to allow consideration for others. This accusation, of course, holds good with history specialists. Unless there is some conscious effort, we shall find that we shall tend to forget that there are opportunities of bringing in good references to other subjects of the school curriculum. This is one of the evils of specialisation. But we are living in an age of specialisation, in educational as in all other matters, and we must do our best to remedy the defects of a system which in its main points is undoubtedly far superior to the old system of all-round form-teachers, at any rate in the case of secondary schools.

What is to be done to remedy this defect? There must be a united effort. It will not do for one teacher only to attempt a system of correlation. Cases have been known where the energy of one teacher has impressed the stamp of his special subject on a whole school; where, for instance, mathematics, manual training, drawing, geography, and languages have all been reduced by the machinations of an enthusiastic history specialist to the position of handmaids to his own subject. An instance of this sort, of course, is rare. If, as should be the case, the majority of the staff are keen upon their own subjects, concessions and compromises will be necessary, and there must be frequent mutual discussions on the syllabus of each subject. Whether these discussions will result in any satisfactory system of correlation will depend on the general ability and common-sense of the staff as a whole; all that can be hoped for is that some manner of compromise may be devised by which the natural relationship between the different subjects may be brought out without provoking any teacher to ill-will with the idea that he must give more than he is allowed to take.

Very intimate indeed is the connection between history and geography. The great physical features of the world have formed the setting for the development of the drama of human progress, while in certain cases the activities of the human race or even of individuals have contributed to considerable alterations in the physical appearance of the surface of the earth. Once more, however, we shall find it necessary to take up arms against the overmighty pretensions of the sectional specialist. There has appeared a school of historical thinkers who attempt to apply to the details of human history the grand principle that geography controls and directs everything. Now these opinions are based on an undoubted truth, namely that physical features do exert a profound influence upon human energy, human character and human activities. But the most extreme of the champions of this school of thought, by carrying their deductions too far into the details of human development, rob their theory of much of its force. By asking too much they challenge a reaction which will act unfavourably upon it. Yet it is fairly obvious that history cannot be properly understood without some knowledge of geography, while geography frequently finds a knowledge of history extremely conducive to its ready interpretation.

The development of any country depends to a great extent on its climate, its natural resources, its proximity to trade-routes, its seaboard and its frontiers. Climate, scenery and meteorological phenomena have a great deal to do with the beliefs and religion of a people. Physical features are a pre-eminent factor in all military operations. Conversely, human effort and energy have in some cases affected and altered the geographical configuration of a country. With the piercing of the Alpine railway tunnels the great central European mountain-system ceases to act as a formidable bar to commerce and communication. The draining of the marshes of the Welland, Nen and Great Ouse has entirely altered the physical appearance of a million acres in the east of England. The construction of the Suez and Panama Canals has revolutionised trade-routes. The Roman Campagna is no longer a pestiferous death-trap to its denizens, and this is entirely due to human causes.

We can emphasise the relationship of geography and history in many ways. Let us quote a few examples. Consider the military geography of the United Kingdom. The barrier of the Pennines and the importance of its gaps is apparent in several instances of historical consequence, notably in William the Conqueror's celebrated march to

Chester and in Prince Rupert's northern campaign of 1644. The two main roads into Scotland have to be mentioned a score of times in the course of our history. The Essex Forest and the Weald profoundly influenced the history of the Anglo-Saxon Kingdoms of Essex and Sussex. The Severn river-basin must be described if we deal with Offa's contest against the Welsh, Buckingham's rebellion of 1483, or the Worcester campaign of 1651. Some knowledge of Irish geography is necessary to understand the campaign of Aughrim. An appreciation of the centres of mineral wealth and manufacturing industry must underlie any understanding of the Reform Bills of 1832, 1867, 1885 and 1917.

It is also important to know the geographical reason for the establishment of important historical cities and towns. It makes an interesting lesson to trace the reason for the existence of the Roman towns of Britain in the particular places in which they are to be found. The military position of a fortress like Carlisle or Guildford or Reigate may be easily explained with the aid of geography; the same thing will apply in the case of places of European consequence like Belfort, Liége, Verona and Cracow.

Another very interesting study is that of place-names. Of course this cannot be carried out at all systematically either in history or in geography lessons, but very important pieces of information may often be elicited from a place-name. Thus it may be discovered that Stamford marks the crossing of the River Welland by the "Stone" road of the Romans, that Carisbrooke is the "Burh" of the Wiht-gara—the dwellers in Wight, that Castle Richard in Herefordshire marks the site of one of the first stone castles in England, built by one of Edward the Confessor's Norman friends, and that Chelsea and Battersea preserve the memory of the days when the Thames at London was a broad and marshy tidal river studded with islands that rose above the fens. The settlements of the Danes can be very well indicated by marking on a map the places now bearing names that terminate in -by and -thorpe.

It will prove, perhaps, impossible to devise a satisfactory correlated syllabus for history and geography, though in some schools the experiment has been tried. A syllabus that works in the geography of Spain for the convenience of the Peninsular War or that arranges lessons on Edward I's Scottish wars to coincide with the teaching of Scottish geography is bound to be artificial and distorted. We can hardly twist our senior history course far out of the broad chronological path, and when the history syllabus is comparatively rigid, we can hardly expect teachers of geography to make all the sacrifices in order to benefit the sister-subject. Correlation will more usually take the form of frequent cross-reference and allusion.

Thus when the history teacher is dealing with English history, he should make frequent use of the map and the lessons to be drawn from its study; in dealing with India he will not forget to mention frequently the physical features and climate of the country. The same applies to America, Australia or wherever the course of the history lesson happens to take him. In a similar way, the geography teacher should be always ready to call attention to historical events and developments which have taken place in the areas with which he happens to be dealing. In this way both subjects will mutually feel the benefits conferred by the study of the one upon the study of the other.

The relationship which exists between history and literature is obvious. The literature of a nation is an expression of its thoughts, its ideals and its aims. No thorough idea of the spirit of a period of history can be obtained without a perusal of the literary products of that time. Though we cannot hope to present to our pupils, or even to get them to read, a very large quantity of the literature of past ages, we should, if possible, see that they get a slight acquaintance with one or two examples of such productions.

It is, however, fairly obvious that the time at the disposal of the history teacher will not allow him to do more than occasionally quote short extracts from contemporary writers. Whatever larger effort is made in this direction must depend on the willing co-operation of the teacher of English. The English teacher will probably be taking with his classes certain long works for more or less complete reading and study, and if it can be arranged that such works shall in some cases be of historical interest and importance and shall also in some cases fit in with contemporary periods being studied at the same time, so much the better. It will depend, however, upon the circumstances guiding the English teacher, how far this form of co-operation can be carried. Where the functions of history teacher and English teacher are combined in the same person there will, of course, be no difficulty in arranging a slightly correlated syllabus.

It would be possible to fill a vast number of pages with suggestions of works which would fulfil the purpose of connecting history and literature. It will be sufficient to indicate a few examples. For the Middle Ages we have Chaucer's "Canterbury Tales," the Prologue of which is of priceless value for the history of the fourteenth century, and Langland's "Piers Plowman," from which suitable passages may be taken. The Shakespearian plays provide material for the Tudor period, with the works of Spenser, Latimer and More. Much good will come from a study of a portion of Hakluyt's "Voyages," now published in a cheap series. Selections from the "Tatler" and the "Spectator" can enliven the reign of Queen Anne, just as Milton can be brought in to illustrate the Puritan movement. The social history of the eighteenth century may be illustrated by Cowper's "Task," by Goldsmith's "Deserted Village," by the works of Lamb and Crabbe, the last of whom, in his "Parish Register" and "Tales of the Borough," gives many interesting side-lights on the conditions of his time.

There are also numerous works of literary value which, though not strictly contemporary, may be used as an aid to the remembering of historical events. A few examples of these may be given. There are poems like Burns' stirring "Scots wha hae," Drayton's "Agincourt," Scott's "Flodden," Tennyson's "Revenge," Macaulay's "Armada" and "Naseby," and Palgrave's "Trafalgar." There are historical novels like Scott's "Ivanhoe" and "Kenilworth," Defoe's "Journal of the Plague Year," Dickens' "Barnaby Rudge" and Thackeray's "Esmond." If a novel of this kind is read through even once only by a class, it will give a very vivid idea of the living force of history.

We now turn to the subject of the correlation of history with woodwork and drawing. This again must depend upon the willingness of the other instructors to adopt historical subjects as models for their work. Though we have little to offer in exchange for assistance thus rendered, it may sometimes be found not inconvenient for drawing and woodwork instructors to adopt historical models.

In the way of woodwork and modelling there are numerous historical subjects which can be taken. Models of clay can be made to illustrate viking ships, mediaeval weapons, cannon and other objects. Wooden models can be made of the stocks, of the guillotine, of siege engines. Very interesting will a study of these last be found. Plans for models can be worked out, with a little care, from pictures such as those in Viollet-le-Duc's "Architecture Militaire."

An example may be given of how a simple model of a siege-engine may be made. The model is that of the *trébuchet*, the pictures of which are generally well known. A base is made by fastening together three stripes of wood in the shape of the letter H; from the points where the strips join, two other strips are raised perpendicularly to act as the supports of the balance-pivot. Between these two uprights, at the distance of several inches from the ground, according to the size of the model constructed, the pivot-beam is placed, and across this is fixed the main throwing-beam, at one end of which there will be fastened the weight, and at the other there will be scooped out, or fastened on, a receptacle for the objects to be thrown. If the pivot is arranged to move smoothy and easily, a hook and a piece of string for the lowering of the receptacle will complete a presentable working-model of a *trébuchet*.

Models may also be made of castles, monasteries and abbeys, but these require a much greater amount of work, and usually a certain amount of collaboration between various pupils. A good way to proceed with a model of this sort is as follows:—First a plan of some actual mediaeval castle is procured, and is copied on a large sheet of blank paper, on the same scale as that on which it is intended the model shall be. When a satisfactory ground-plan has been made, it can be pasted or pinned on to a wooden base, which will serve as the ground from which the model is to be raised. Small plans are then drawn out with the measurements and instructions for each particular section of curtain wall, each turret and each building, every pupil taking charge of one unit. These separate pieces, when completely made and painted, may then be brought together and glued or otherwise fixed on the board. The painting may often be profitably delayed until the whole model has been put together.

Plans of castles and religious buildings may be found in works such as the before-named book of Viollet-le-Duc and Barnard's "Companion to Mediaeval History," or in local guide-books.

In drawing there is much, of course, which can be done to illustrate history lessons. Arms and armour often make good subjects for drawing, while in the field of decorative design we can not only use the ornamentations drawn from architectural models but coats of arms as well. The study of heraldry, though interesting, can have no place in the history syllabus, but it would be a useful thing if, in drawing and colouring designs, pupils could get to know the coats of arms of the great mediaeval families.

A word may be said, perhaps, on the subject of architecture. A little knowledge of this subject will do a great deal to increase interest in history. If it is not arranged that some information about architecture is given in connection with drawing lessons, then, at least in a secondary school, a few lessons should be devoted by the history teacher to some simple explanations of the greatest developments and changes in British architecture, especially if such changes can be illustrated by examples drawn from the neighbourhood of the school itself.

III. LIBRARIES AND COLLECTIONS

Mr Keatinge points out in "The New Teaching" that the function of the laboratory in relation to science work is represented in history work by the library. Without a good collection of books, advanced work in the upper forms is reduced within very narrow limits. Every school that takes the teaching of history seriously should possess a collection of books on historical subjects. And this should be no mere agglomeration of text-books, source-books, atlases and fortuitous "specimen copies"; it must be a well thought-out collection designed to illustrate and to aid the work laid down in the syllabus, as well as to provide material for private reading on the part of advanced pupils.

As to the composition of this library much might be said, and the books to be purchased for it naturally depend very largely on the funds available for the purpose. A historical library must grow slowly, and we can only indicate roughly the lines on which it can best be brought together.

First we must have certain books which may be termed volumes of general reference, detailed Histories of England and Europe and such like books. Of long series of volumes on the history of England there are several, notably Longman's "Political History of England" in twelve volumes, and Methuen's "History of England" in seven. In European History there are also several series, notably the "Periods of European History" series published by Rivington and on a very much larger scale the Cambridge Mediaeval and Modern Histories, which include chapters on English history. As regards other more general reference books, there is a Dictionary of English History published by Cassell, while there is an excellent little Biographical Dictionary published by Chambers. An historical atlas, which need not be too expensive, should also be added to the library. Keith Johnson's and Gardiner's are both good and cheap.

During recent years there have appeared several series of cheap reprints of famous books of the Everyman type. The historical volumes of these series are often of such importance that, at their low price, we can have no excuse for failing to get them. A short list of such books may be given: The "Anglo-Saxon Chronicle," Bede's "History of the English Church," Thierry's "Norman Conquest," Giraldus Cambrensis' "Itinerary of Wales," Stanley's "Memorials of Canterbury," Froude's "History of England," Macaulay's "History of England," Pepys' "Diary," Evelyn's "Diary," Cromwell's "Letters," Burnet's "History of His Own Time," Parkman's "Montcalm" and "Wolfe," Macaulay's "Essays," Pitt's "Orations," Burke's "Orations"—these are but a few of the volumes on English historical subjects issued in one series alone—the "Everyman." From the same series we may draw the following works on European History: Gibbon's "Decline and Fall of the Roman Empire," Sismondi's "Italian Republics," Lützow's "History of Bohemia," Machiavelli's "History of Florence," Motley's "Dutch Republic," Carlyle's "French Revolution," and other volumes. Nelson's shilling series supplies some good historical books, such as Morley's "Life of Cobden" and Bagehot's "British Constitution." There are other important French volumes of historical import in their shilling French series, such as Lévy's "Napoléon Intime" and Ségur's "Campagne de Russie." Other historical works can be found in Bohn's cheap reprints, in the World's Classics series and in other similar collections. A little more expensive is Fisher Unwin's half-crown series, which includes Seignobos' interesting volumes on "Civilisation," Villari's "Life and Times of Machiavelli" and some of Thorold Rogers' books on "Economic History."

A word must be said for the new modern series issued by the "Home University" editors, the "People's Books" and the Cambridge University Handbooks. With few exceptions these brief modern works, written by historical experts, are excellent handbooks for elementary historical study. In all such cases, where the book in question is modern and without a seasoned reputation, it is well for the teacher to have a glance through it before deciding on its usefulness for his school library.

As for the more expensive historical books, one can hardly say offhand what volumes should be recommended for inclusion. Individual teachers will doubtless differ as to the particular books they consider indispensable, and it would probably be unwise to put forward the names of any, merely on the strength of their general reputation. The specialist will doubtless be acquainted with the general run of historical literature and, unless the amount of money at his disposal be very great indeed, he will probably be at no loss to indicate suitable additions.

If a school possesses a good historical library, it may be used with effect, not merely for the use and reference of the teacher, who will find in it ready to hand the materials for illustrating his lessons, but for the use and reference of the pupils as well. It will be employed in connection with those lessons in which senior pupils are set to get up historical subjects, and no opportunity should be allowed to pass by in which they may be encouraged to read for themselves, out of school-hours, the great historical masterpieces.

Besides collecting a library of historical volumes, it will also be advisable to make a collection of pictures which may illustrate the subjects with which we deal. These pictures may be obtained from a number of sources. Certain publishers issue short series of wall-pictures illustrating subjects drawn from history. These pictures usually prove somewhat expensive, particularly if they are going to be preserved by framing. Other pictures, notably historical portraits and reproductions of famous pictures, may be obtained from firms of engravers and picture-shops. These carefully-prepared and in many cases very artistic productions make very fitting ornaments for the school-room wall, but their purchase on a large scale is not altogether advisable. If pupils hold their history lessons in a room which is always surrounded with pictures, they soon begin to take these pictures as a matter of course and lose interest in them. Familiarity in this case undoubtedly breeds contempt. It will be found more effective to keep the majority of our pictures in store and only to bring them out to illustrate our lessons directly. They can then be left for display in the class-room for some time, and then, when other pictures have come along to replace them, they may be taken down and reserved for the next year's use. This will be found to be far better than keeping them always before the pupil's eyes.

A collection of historical pictures may also be got together by the pupils themselves. A class should always be encouraged to bring to school any illustrations that pupils may get hold of to illustrate their lessons. These may come from books, magazines and even sometimes from advertisement bills; the humble cigarette card, too, is not to be despised. Again, there is much to be done with a collection of picture postcards. Every history teacher should make a school collection of this form of illustration. Historical postcards may be got together from all sorts of places. There are cards of celebrated pictures, cards of portraits in the National Portrait Gallery, cards of historic buildings and scenes, representations of famous documents. When the boys or girls go for their holidays in the summer, they should be asked to collect postcards of anything of historical interest in the district to which they happen to go. It is remarkable what good results will come from the beginning of a postcard collection of this description.

Cards and magazine-pictures can often be shown to great advantage if they can be mounted on thick paper or thin cardboard, giving some slight margin round them, on which it is sometimes good to write explanatory notes on the pictures. If the wall of the schoolroom does not present an extensive wooden surface on which illustrations may be fixed with drawing pins, a couple of wooden grooves may be constructed round the walls, and into these wooden grooves may be slipped pieces of cardboard on which the pictures can be pinned or otherwise mounted.

The history-room should certainly possess one or two large wall-maps. These should be chosen to illustrate those areas in which most historical action has taken place. A physical map shaded to represent contours will frequently be found more useful than a political map, though in this case the teacher will have to make sure of the exact position of places discussed before dealing with the map. There should certainly be a map of England and Wales, and a larger one of the United Kingdom; a map of the latter will prove more effective than two larger maps of Scotland and Ireland. Then it will be useful to have a large wall-map of France, again preferably a physical map, for in the Middle Ages much of our history is concerned with France, and the map will frequently have to be used. For European history, and even for English history, a map of Europe will be required; the difficulties connected with the difference in the political configuration at different periods can again best be obviated by having a physical map.

All models made by the pupils should find a place in the history store-cupboard, being brought out to illustrate one point or another when it crops up; duplicate specimens of models need not, of course, as a general rule be retained at school. Drawings and paintings should also find a place here, and should always bear the name of the pupil responsible for them as well as the name of the school in which they were made.

A word or two may be said on the subject of lantern-slides and lantern-lessons. Nothing helps to make the past real in the eyes of the pupil so much as the presentation of visual images by means of large pictures. But considerations of space and the great cost which is entailed in the acquisition of a large collection of good-sized pictures will prevent many schools from attempting to form such a gallery. The same function may be as effectively or even more effectively fulfilled by lantern-slides, for the effect of the darkened room, and the consequent focussing of all visual activity upon the picture on the screen, are more favourable to mental concentration on the picture than the conditions governing the display of a picture in an ordinary lighted room.

Some schools possess facilities for this sort of work, while others do not. Where a lantern exists, an occasional lantern-lesson is a relief from the ordinary lessons, but we should not make it of too frequent occurrence; lantern-shows are always apt to lose force by constant repetition. Unless a school has plenty of money to spare, it will not be possible to obtain a very large collection of lantern-slides, though in some districts, such as for example the County of London, schools may subscribe to a circulating library of lantern-slides, and this, of course, is a decided advantage. It will often be found useful to get the class to describe the slides as they appear on the screen, if they illustrate work already done.

Books, drawings, pictures, postcards, models, maps and lantern-slides will make an excellent school historical collection. Every teacher should take the opportunity of also building up a collection of good past work done by his pupils, for his own satisfaction, for the credit of his school, and for the inspiration of future pupils. The inclusion of some piece of his work in the collection should be made the aim and ambition of every boy or girl who studies the subject of history in the school.

IV. *CAVENDO TUTUS*

It remains, in a few brief remarks, to call attention to some of the most common pitfalls which beset the instructor of this subject.

In the first place it cannot be too often repeated that the teacher should never lose sight of his main plan. Particularly in the senior forms, he must keep himself from making too wide excursions beyond the bounds of the syllabus. It is quite possible that with an intelligent class, one that is prone to ask numerous questions, he will find himself being led away into lengthy expatiation on subjects which do not fall well within the bounds of the lesson. Time should certainly be allotted to a lesson on military equipments at the time of the Civil War of 1642, but we should not allow a lesson on the course of the Marston Moor campaign to be interrupted by questions relative to muskets and pikes. The religious question in the Ireland of William of Orange's time calls for some discussion, but we must not be led off into premature remarks about the recent Home Rule question.

Again, facts should not be piled up with the idea of filling out a lesson. Some teachers have a way of rolling out incidents and pieces of information without connection and without definite aim, in a manner that has been described as "bead-stringing." If facts that are not essential to the main story of history are being given, it ought to be with the definite idea of illustrating the more important facts or of impressing them on the minds of the pupils.

Another great fault of history teachers is that they are

frequently addicted to moralising on events. In the case of some instructors, almost every fresh phase of an historical episode is made the occasion for a more or less dithyrambic exposition of the virtue or otherwise of the characters concerned.

Anything which touches upon the sphere of pure ethics is far better left to the discussion of the class, and it will often prove useful to encourage an informal debate on some such topic. Moralising on events which have already been outlined is in most cases a waste of energy on the part of the teacher, but a useful exercise in expressing themselves and a useful aid to remembering the facts for the pupils.

There is, however, one species of moralising which commands more excuse and which in many cases is deliberately encouraged by authority. This is the cult of patriotism. English schools are not subjected to State regulation in this respect. In some other countries, however, there is a distinct attempt on the part of the State to colour the course of instruction in history with a strong national bias. Thus in France the State schools are expected to encourage the love of *la patrie* and an admiration for the institutions and principles of the Republic. In Germany instructions were issued that history teachers should inculcate the principles of German patriotism, the necessity of German unity and the virtues of the dynasty. The same sort of thing was apparent in the State instructions issued both in the Austrian and in the Hungarian schools. In the British Colonies, too, the instruction has a distinctly Imperial tendency, bringing out as far as possible the advantages of the unity of the Empire and encouraging the strengthening of the ties which bind the Colonies to the mother-country. So it is obvious that the cult of patriotism is very widely practised in schools outside these islands. It would take much space to discuss the advisability of establishing some such system in British schools but we may perhaps not be considered wrong in saying that the cult of patriotism in our history lessons is far from being a fault.

Although the remark applies equally to all subjects, it may be as well to be on our guard against getting over the heads of our pupils. Language and ideas must be proportioned to the capacity of the class for understanding them, and we must neither fall into the habit of using too advanced words nor embark upon too advanced and complex political ideas. The teacher should always try and picture to himself the mental attitude of the pupils, to put himself in their place, and so to gauge the effect of his lessons. It must not be forgotten, either, that frequent tests are necessary in order to estimate what progress the class is making in the acquisition of solid knowledge. Furthermore, we must always see to it that in dealing with past ages we really do bring out the essential differences between old and new institutions and ideas. It is no good talking about the Parliament of Edward I and of Charles I unless we have explained how the assemblies of those reigns were not the same as the modern Parliaments; it is no good speaking of the Roman Catholic religion of the Middle Ages unless we have made sure that our pupils have rid themselves of the idea of the present day religious system in England, where all creeds exist side by side in peace and mutual toleration. In the second place we must not fall into the temptation of holding up past manners and facts to ridicule; it is easy and natural for us to laugh at the passionate and emotional conduct of earlier centuries and at their somewhat crude table-habits, it is easy for us to sneer at the diminutive size of the armies that fought at Agincourt and Blenheim compared with our modern hosts, but we shall not be pursuing the right line if we encourage this kind of "superior" and contemptuous attitude towards the past. It is our task to try to understand our ancestors, not to sneer at them. It has been frequently asserted that our ordinary history deals too much with men and too little with mankind. A deeper charge still we often hear brought against our historians. It is asserted that the history we learn at school and in the university is superficial, that it deals only with the surface layer of human life, with the kings and princes and statesmen instead of with the merchants and farmers and workmen, with the generals and admirals instead of with the soldiers and sailors, with parliamentary debates and political intrigues, and not with the price of bread and conditions of home life. This charge too is based upon truth, for until quite recently social and economic history has taken a very humble place in the syllabus of both school and university. Now one of the virtuous faculties which a study of history is supposed to bring out is a power of discerning the tendency to exaggeration displayed by advocates of rival policies and opinions; and if this be so, it is to be hoped that the student will be able to avoid the adoption of either the political or the social idea of history teaching in their extreme form. Of course we cannot neglect the masses in our historical researches; the state of public opinion, the standard of civilisation, the economic needs of the community, the pressure of unemployment and hunger, the religious beliefs of the people are factors of profound significance, the factors, indeed, on which all other historical influences are based. But here again we must utter a twofold warning. The cardinal faults of the social-economic school of history teachers are that they devote far too much time to their own social and economic side of history and that they load up their material with an overheavy mass of trivial detail, equalling if not surpassing the sins of the old-fashioned political school in this respect.

On the principle of devoting more attention to those movements of history that concern large masses of men than to those that concern smaller numbers, perhaps the social aspect of historical study seems to command a much larger amount of attention than the political. But another consideration cuts across this in a rather forcible way. The elementary factors of human life remain the same through all ages, and social and economic history deal largely with these elementary factors. Men must always eat, they must always dress in mild and cool climates, they must always find means of amusing themselves in their spare hours. Food may differ from time to time, clothes and fashions may alter, sports and pastimes may change with the passing centuries, but their general characteristics remain the same, and it is not a matter of great importance whether the people dress in red or blue or black, in ruffs or starched collars, or whether they play nine men morris and clash or cricket and football and billiards. The general social condition of the people remains very much the same from age to age; it is only in times of extraordinary development, such as those of the Industrial Revolution, that the social condition undergoes a serious change. It will thus be found that the main outlines of social history can be written in comparatively few pages, or taught in comparatively few lessons. Not so the political outlines; the institutions under which the people are governed require greater explanation to those pupils who, while easily understanding social references, have no knowledge or experience of the working of political institutions; these institutions too change more rapidly than the social conditions on which they are primarily based. It is true that the political commotions of history are largely superficial, but they are nevertheless important when they produce great results, and it will take very much longer for the teacher to explain the political movements than to explain the contemporary social changes. For instance, no one would deny the real importance of the struggle between Crown and Parliament in the seventeenth century; but when we have sketched the social conditions of 1603 we have virtually also sketched those of 1625 and 1640 and 1660 and 1689. Things had not moved so very rapidly in the social world, except when they reflected the political disturbances, as in connection with the religious changes engineered by Roundheads and Cavaliers. On the other hand the political movements of that time, the conflicts between the Kings and the Parliaments, the movements of armies in the Civil War, the laws passed by triumphant parties, all these require quite a considerable amount of space and time devoted to them.

We see then that it is possible to compress our social and economic history into a very much smaller compass than we can our political history and thus, while granting the claim of the former to a prominent place in the syllabus, reason demands that political and constitutional subjects should command the greater part of the time at our disposal.

Again, those social economic enthusiasts who clamour loudest against the trivial personalities of Piers Gaveston, Anne Boleyn and George Villiers are often found plunging headlong into the same abyss, *mutato nomine*. Quite unimportant details about miracle plays and ten-course banquets and court fashions fulfil the same *rôle* in their social histories as the above mentioned characters filled in the old fashioned political histories. These things are all doubtless very interesting, but so are the private lives of celebrities and we must treat both in the same way. As a means of stimulating historical interest, as a means of illustrating the more important facts, as an occasional layer of jam in the plain pudding of the school history-lesson, they have their value; but in both cases we must never forget the true proportion of their historical importance.

History and biography are closely allied subjects but they are not the same. History deals with nations. Biography deals with individuals. The subjects may be closely cognate; nations are often profoundly influenced by the thoughts and actions of a great individual; conversely great men and women draw much of their inspiration and all their opportunity from the society into which they are thrown by Providence. But in teaching one, we must beware of rambling off into the other, although we may sometimes enlist the services of the sister-subject in order to facilitate history teaching. There is no doubt much that is fascinating in the lives of such great men as William the Conqueror, Thomas Becket, Martin Luther, Wellington, Nelson, Napoleon; but in teaching of these men it must not be forgotten that we are dealing with their influence on the nation and not with their own personal history. The biographical tradition is very strong in history teaching, and finds its worst expression in the once universal division of the history book into reigns, each chapter being labelled with the name of one of the sovereigns.

Once again we must take warning. We must not lose sight of the solid work which we expect our pupils to do. It is not enough that we should entertain and amuse, it is not enough that we should find occupation for the minds of our classes, we must secure real effort and real accomplishment. It is quite possible to get excellent specimens of work done in the way of maps and exercises and compositions, without their yielding any very deep or permanent results in the way of facts and ideas remembered. Some teachers are apt to lose sight of this in their pursuit of the more refined methods of instruction.

Another similar fault is that of doing much of the work for the pupil that should be done by him. Wherever it is possible for a class to extract information from the text-book it should never be told by the teacher; wherever a fact can be elicited from the class itself, it should not come from the teacher's lips. But these are faults which apply to the teaching of almost all subjects, and are not confined to teachers of history.

An energetic history teacher has to be a person of manifold activities. Not only has he to carry out his ordinary school work, to prepare lessons, to correct exercises, to plan and conduct school visits; he has to keep in touch with his subject in a variety of other ways. He must keep his eye on the educational papers, and seize upon any fresh ideas on history-teaching therein put forward. He has to read, in his own private time, a great deal of historical matter, to amplify and add to his knowledge. He ought to look out for reviews of new historical works in the columns of the Press. He should, if possible, join and attend the meetings of some such society as the Historical Association. In short, it is only a specialist who can make a thoroughly good teacher of this subject.

It is the duty of a military commander to be ever alert and active, keeping his eye on his front, his flank, his rear, on his train of supplies, on the condition of the weather, on a vast number of other things. So it is with the history-teacher. It used to be at one time a prevalent idea that history was one of the easiest of all subjects to teach. It was only necessary, it was thought, to get hold of a text-book and keep a page or two ahead of the class, and there was an end of it. But it ought to be apparent by this time that this is very far from the truth. History is perhaps the most difficult of all the subjects of the school curriculum to teach with effect. It requires a teacher who is willing to be ever active, ever enquiring, ever on his guard against the numerous pitfalls which beset his path. He may well take as his motto that of one of our ducal houses, *Cavendo tutus*.

V. SPECIMEN LESSONS

OUTLINE sketch of three specimen lessons, for junior classes, age 11–13. These lessons may be spread out over a series of shorter lessons if desired; in fact it is preferable that they should be so extended.

(a) *The Norman Conquest.*

(This lesson will keep very closely to pure narrative, with little in the way of digression.)

Edward the Confessor—his character—where he spent his youth—his Norman friends—they are placed in offices of power in England—a court filled with Normans.

Irritation of the English nobles—but they are distracted by their own quarrels—Godwin and Harold; Edwin and Morcar—the Dover incident (Eustace of Boulogne)—Godwin takes the part of the Dover men, and is banished—*William's visit to England*—Godwin returns, a general rebellion, the nobles force Edward to expel his Norman favourites.

Harold becomes leading minister—his shipwreck in Ponthieu—*William secures his liberty and persuades him to take the oath*—death of King Edward—meeting of the Witan—possible candidates: Edgar Atheling, Danish and Scandinavian princes, William of Normandy, Harold—Harold secures his own election—*anger of William, he resolves on war*, 1066.

Two invasions preparing—Harold Hardrada and his fleet—William's difficult task—the Norman barons refuse to fight—*he collects a volunteer army*—men arrive from all parts of France—he promises them great rewards. A third set of plotters: Edwin and Morcar would prefer Edgar Atheling as King—Harold's danger threefold:—(*a*) Norwegians, (*b*) Normans, (*c*) dissatisfied English nobles.

Hardrada's invasion—Tostig joins him—the landing—Edwin and Morcar beaten at Fulford—Harold arrives—victory of Stamford Bridge—great rejoicings—*news of William's landing.*

Harold marches south—Edwin and Morcar's slackness—their probable treason—they have little interest in Wessex—William's camp at Hastings—*the two armies advance—battle of Senlac* (details)—death of Harold.

The contest now between *only two claimants, Edgar and William*—Edgar declared King by Edwin and Morcar—William advances on London, fails to secure the bridge—he makes a wide march round London—advances down the Watling Street—Edwin and Morcar overawed—they submit—*Treaty of Berkhampstead—William enters London and is crowned King*—distribution of land and rewards to the victorious army.

NOTE. The important stages in the development of the main theme of the story are shown in italics.

(*b*) *A Feudal Village.*

(This lesson does not centre round an event or series of events. It is merely descriptive of society in a thirteenth-century village, and gives in an essay form some ideas respecting mediaeval land-tenure, military service, etc.)

The average village small—usually a manor—there is a lord, his house, his steward—the people divided into villeins and freemen—most of them villeins—what it meant to be a villein—cannot leave the village, marry, sell beasts, cut down trees, without lord's consent—no share in government—no right to bring lawsuits against others, except in his lord's own court.

How the soil was tilled—the three-field system—wheat, barley and fallow—how the three areas were distributed, rarely each in one piece—every villager must have his share of land, in wheat and barley—rotation of crops causes constant change of pieces under cultivation—cases of a fresh distribution each year—the strip system—each villager has many little strips—advantages of the change system; its disadvantages.

Some villagers hold more than others—superior position of the freemen—big share held by lord of the manor—how did he get this big estate cultivated?

Rents of the villeins—service—produce—money—rents of the "socage freemen"—service—produce and money—other varieties of rent; services in the lord's hall, butler, steward, falconer, chamberlain (grand serjeanty)—gifts and nominal rent (petty serjeanty)—prayers and masses of the Church for the lord's soul (frank almoign). Lastly, the military tenant (knight service).

How the King's army was raised—partly by hire, partly by rent agreement (military tenure)—a "knight's fee"—what the service was.

Other features of the mediaeval village—the church—its uses, religious and secular—the lord's mill and dovecote—usual obligation on some villager to attend hundred and shire courts.

Land round the village—meadow strips—waste lands—right to pasture animals and cut turf, etc.—"parks" and "bocland."

(c) *Nelson and his Ships.*

(This lesson will take Nelson as the central figure, will give a brief outline of his public life, and will bring in a good deal of detail concerning the old navy.)

Horatio Nelson—early life—takes to the sea—ships of the eighteenth century—skill needed to manage them—long voyages—water and food supplies—scurvy.

The Navy—dress and pay of officers and men—recruitment—the press gang—the lash.

Methods of fighting—prize money—British naval supremacy—our chief enemies—battle of St Vincent; Nelson's share—naval tactics—"breaking the line"—Nelson in command in the Mediterranean—battle of the Nile—expedition to seize the Danish fleet—battle of Copenhagen—Nelson's captains and brother admirals—Hood, Collingwood, Calder, Howe, Jervis, Duncan.

The last naval campaign of Nelson—Napoleon's invasion plan—Villeneuve lures Nelson to the West Indies—the return—Villeneuve foiled by Calder—he is disgraced, but resolves to fight before he is dismissed—Trafalgar—details of the battle and of Nelson's death—results of Trafalgar—Nelson's work for England—his famous signal.

VI. SHORT BIBLIOGRAPHY

A short bibliography of useful and easily accessible literature on the Teaching of History.

[A very full bibliography of this subject will be found in the Appendices to Professor H. Johnson's *Teaching of History* (Macmillan, 1915). His bibliography includes many French and German works.

An early work on the subject is J. Wyer's *Bibliography of the study and teaching of History*, published in America in 1899, though naturally this book is somewhat obsolete from the modern methodologist's point of view.]

Report of the Committee of Seven. *The Study of History in Schools.* New York. 1899.

Essays on the Teaching of History. Cambridge. 1901.

H. L. Withers. *The Teaching of History* and other papers. Manchester. 1904.

H. B. George. *The Relations of Geography and History.* Oxford. 1907.

B. Hinsdale. *How to study and teach History.* New York. 1908.

Circular 599. Board of Education. London. 1908.

J. W. Allen. *The Place of History in Education.* London. 1909.

Report of the Committee of Eight. *The Study of History in Elementary Schools.* New York. 1909.

M. W. Keatinge. *Studies in the Teaching of History.* London. 1910.

H. Bourne. *The Teaching of History and Civics.* New York. 1910.

Report on the Teaching of History in the London Elementary Schools. London. 1911.

Report of the Committee of Eight. *The Teaching of History in Secondary Schools.* New York. 1911.

W. F. Bliss. *History in the Elementary Schools.* New York. 1911.

E. C. Hartwell. *The Teaching of History.* Boston. 1913.

O. Jäger. *The Teaching of History.* (American translation, Chicago. 1915.)

H. Johnson. *Teaching of History in Elementary and Secondary Schools.* London. 1915.

J. Archer. *The Teaching of History.* Manchester. 1916.

C. H. Jarvis. *The Teaching of History.* Oxford. 1917.

J. W. Adamson. *History* in *The Practice of Instruction.* London. 1912.

INDEX

For EU product safety concerns, contact us at Calle de José Abascal, 56–1°, 28003 Madrid, Spain or eugpsr@cambridge.org.

www.ingramcontent.com/pod-product-compliance
Ingram Content Group UK Ltd.
Pitfield, Milton Keynes, MK11 3LW, UK
UKHW020313140625
459647UK00018B/1854

* 9 7 8 1 1 0 7 6 2 1 8 9 3 *